COIN-COLLECTING IN NORTHERN INDIA

COIN-COLLECTING IN NORTHERN INDIA

CHARLES. J. RODGERS

GYAN

Published by

GYAN

Gyan Publishing House
5, Ansari Road
Daryaganj, New Delhi-110002
Phone: 011-47034999, 9811692060
E-mail: books@gyanbooks.com

Distribution Network
gyanbooks.com
India, USA, Canada, UK, Australia, France

ISBN : 978-81-212-3253-1 (PB)
First Published, 1894

2nd Impression 2020

Printed at: Gyan Press, Delhi.

Coin-Collecting in Northern India
Author: Charles. J. Rodgers

COIN-COLLECTING

IN

NORTHERN INDIA

BY

CHARLES J. RODGERS

HONORARY NUMISMATIST TO THE GOVERNMENT OF INDIA.

ALLAHABAD

PRINTED AT THE PIONEER PRESS

1894

KEY TO PLATES.

PLATE I.

Different kinds of silver punch-marked coins.—Pali names of Eukratides, Apollodotus and Azilises.—Pali titles for Maharaja, Rajadiraja and Righteous.

PLATE II.

Coin
(1) Copper coin of Apollodotus.
(2) " " " legend in straight lines.
(3) Square copper coin of Menander.
(4) " " " Strato.
(5) " " " " 2nd type.
(6) Copper coin of Zoilus.
(7) Silver coin of Telephus.
(8) Square copper coin of Hippostratus.
(9) Silver didrachma of "
(10) Square copper coin of Manes.
(11) " " " Azes.
(12) Copper coin of Abdagases.
(13) " " " 2nd type.

PLATE III.

(1) Copper coin of Pasuta Jaya of Kashmir.
(2) " " Aditya "
(3) " " Malla Raja "
(4) " " Raja Roja "
(5) " " Gulhana "
(6) " " Paramana "

These six coins are published now for the first time.

Coin
(1) Square silver coin of Sikandar Shah of Kashmir.
(2) " " " Zain-ul-Abidin "
(3) " " " Hasan Shah "
(5) " " " Muhammad Shah "
(7) " " " Fath Shah "
(9) " " " Nadir Shah "
(14) " " " Humayun Shah "
(15) " " " Islam Shah "

PLATE IV.

(1) Gold coin of Muhammad bin Sam, 1st Sultan of Dehli.
(2) Silver coin of Muhammad bin Sam and his elder brother Gyas-ud-din bin Sam.
(3) Silver coin of Ala-ud-din of Khwarizm.
(4) " " " " 2nd type.
(5) Copper coin of " "
(6) " " " " 2nd type.
(7) Rupee of Shams-ud-din Altamsh.
(8) " " " 2nd type.
(9) Copper coin of " "
(10) " " " " 2nd type.
(11) " " " " 3rd type.
(12) Mohur of Gyas-ud-din Balban.
(13) Rupee of Jalal-ud-din Firoz Shah.

PLATE V.

(1) Silver coin of Babar, struck at Agra.
(2) " " Humayun " Lahore.
(3) " " "
(4) Rupee of Humayun.
(5) " Sher Shah Suri.
(6) " " another type.
(7) Mohur of Islam Shah Suri.
(8) Rupee of Muhammad Shah Suri.
(9) " Sikandar Shah Suri.
(10) Thin silver coin of Akbar, struck at Lahore.
(11) Rupee of Akbar, struck at Dehli.
(12) Mohur of Akbar, struck at Jaunpur.
(13) Rupee of Akbar with his creed on it.

PLATE VI.

Coin
(1) Nisar of Jahangir, struck at Ahmadabad.
(2) ,, ,, ,, Ajmere.
(3) ,, ,, ,, Agra.
(4) Rupee of Shah Jahan, struck at Akbarabad.
(5) Nisar of ,, ,, Kashmir.
(6) ,, ,, ,, Lahore.
(7) Rupee of Aurangzeb, ,, Zafarabad.
(8) ,, Murad Bakhsh, ,, Kambay.
(9) ,, Shah Shujaa.
(10) ,, Kam Bakhsh, struck at Bijapur.
(11) ,, Nadir Shah, ,, Dehli.
(12) Mohur of Ahmad Shah Durrani, struck at Dehli.
(13) Rupee of Muhammad Shah, ,, Masulipatam.
(14) ,, Rafia-ud Darajat, ,, Akbarabad.

Nos. 4, 7, 12, 13 and 14 are published here for the first time.

ERRATA ET CORRIGENDA.

Page 17, 12th line from bottom, for "Shabbazgurhi,"					read	*Shahbazgurhi.*
,,	19, 15th	,,	,,	for "Diglo,"	,,	*Diglot.*
,,	72, 14th	,,	,,	for "Nazir,"	,,	*Nasir.*
,,	93, 12th	,,	,,	for "Muhammad Mahmud,"	,,	*Muhammad, Mahmud.*
,,	95, 7th	,,	,,	for "Hiran,"	,,	*Hisar.*
,,	114, 17th	,,	,,	for "Dara-jat,"	,,	*Darajat.*

PREFACE.

AT the request of many of our subscribers we have reprinted in book form the articles which appeared in the *Pioneer* on COIN-COLLECTING IN NORTHERN INDIA. These articles were, as was surmised at the time of their appearance, by Mr. Charles J. Rodgers, Honorary Numismatist to the Government of India. An additional article has been written, and a list of works on the coins of the Northern India and the adjoining countries up to date, and six plates of illustrations of coins, several hitherto unpublished, have also been added. Mr. Rodgers's residence of over thirty years in Amritsar has made him acquainted with most of the series of coins which at different times were struck in Northern India, and in this book he gives in a condensed form the result of his researches by way of guidance to those who are inclined to take up the fascinating subject of Indian numismatics. Residents of many years' standing will be astonished at the many varieties of coins described. Visitors to India cannot do better than consult its pages before purchasing "Indian portable antiquities." Officers interested in the study of the history of the country of their adoption will find in it much that is new and interesting. The general reader will obtain much necessary information from it, and the student of history will find in it a safe guide in the choice of original documents in metal on which the history of some parts of the story of India is dependent, or by which the history of obscure parts can be more fully illustrated.

COIN COLLECTING IN NORTHERN INDIA.

I.

SOME time ago in going through the bazar of one of our large commercial towns, I noticed a money-changer seated behind a large heap of cowries and a vast array of ordinary pice piled up in four anna piles, ready for changing into silver! Besides his cowries and his change, I noticed that he had also pyramids of other copper coins. Being naturally of an inquisitive turn of mind, I desired permission to examine the pyramid. Permission was at once granted, and I turned over every coin of the heap, which contained at least a thousand. Behind the money-changer I noticed many bags which, upon inquiry, proved to be full of the same kind of coins as were in the pyramid—coins of dynasties long since passed away, or of towns far distant from the one in which I was. I should not like to say how many kinds of coins the pyramid contained. Having a fair knowledge of the vernaculars and of the characters in which they are written, I commenced sorting the coins. To my astonishment the number of kinds approached fifty. The names of the kings on them were not quite so numerous, for I found the same name on coins of different make and size. Still I think the kings were about forty in number. As I remembered reading somewhere or other that the first act of an Eastern sovereign on coming to the throne was to strike coins in his own name, I began to think that in this heap of coins I saw the results of the commands of kings. On further examining the coins I found that not only were the kings' names on them, but the dates and the names of the places of mintage. So I came to this natural conclusion that every piece of copper before me must have been struck *by some king, in some place, and in some year* or other.

I purchased two or three coins of each kind and took them home for further study. I was pretty well up in the history of India, for I considered when I first came to India that it was a shameful thing to live in a country and not know something of its history. On the coins, however, I found names of kings that I had not before seen. Fortunately for me at that time I came across, at a second-hand bookstall, a copy of Prinsep's Tables, in which I found lists of kings who had at any time reigned over any province or principality in the whole of India. This was a godsend indeed. I took my coins and read the names on them, and then looked up the names in Prinsep. I found then that the pyramid of coins was a historical treasure-house, a place where the only records of many kings are to be found. I again visited the money-changer and again made purchases. After a while, when he and I were great friends, and when he found that he was generally richer after my visits, I asked him to show me some of the treasures in the back ground of his shop. He willingly consented, and brought forward an old heavy bag full of coins, and also an old greasy earthen vessel. The contents of both were poured on the shop-floor, and while the money-changer attended to his business of giving cowries for pice and pice for silver and *vice versâ*, I sat on the ground engaged in picking out coins I had not previously purchased. These I as before took home, and after a bath and a change of garments (I suspected that I might be richer entomologically as well as numismatically), I again sat down to read and study my new purchases. I was often stumped, but I made it a rule never to be conquered by any difficulty. I simply acknowledged my ignorance, and set to work to try and find out who had struck each coin I had, and when and where. After a while I extended my acquaintance with the money-changers of the city and found that at first they were all afraid of showing me their coins, but when they found in me a constant purchaser, they were always ready to show me anything they had. Not satisfied with this I paid visits to towns in the vicinity and made the acquaintance of money-changers there. Still not being satisfied I visited towns and cities hundreds of miles away and examined the stores of the money-changers in every one of them. At last I was pretty well known in each one of them, and I only had to present myself before a shop to have all its stores at once displayed to me.

Hitherto I had only purchased copper coins, my means being limited and my home expenses very heavy. It seems that, as a matter of course, I began to know the *sarrafs*, the gentlemen who deal in bullion and who trade in silver and gold coins now no longer current. They sit behind heaps of rupees instead of pyramids of copper coins. They, too, have their bags and their stores. In the bags are silver and gold in every possible shape,—old gold and silver lace, old jewels, cakes of gold and silver, or jewels melted down, ingots of gold from the banks of England, wedge-like lumps of silver from China, boat-like lumps of the same metal from the same country, and gold and silver coins from every nation under the sun that ever had a gold and silver coinage. I do not say that every *sarraf* had all these riches, but this was what I found out might be obtained at these shops.

When at home once on furlough I was shown a house, the owner of which was afflicted with a collecting mania. He did not, however, go to bankers and money-changers and Eastern bazaars for precious things wherewith to fill his cabinets. He made the acquaintance of the hangman, and he purchased from him the ropes he used in removing from this world of crime the people consigned to his hands on the gallows. I often thought about that collection, and I could see that if the collector of execution ropes labelled each one and worked out the whole story of the crime which demanded the execution, his museum must have been a very interesting addition to the Newgate Calendar.

In collecting coins, however, the collector is supposed not to be afflicted with a mania of any kind, but only with a desire to extend his own knowledge and that of others. First of all, he finds out the names of the kings who struck the coins. These, it will be answered, the histories give us. Do they ? Not in all cases. In the East, history has never in many countries been written. Coins and inscriptions are the only histories. In the East, if the histories were written, they were often garbled. Whether the histories were written or were not, it is always interesting to handle money which we know must have been in use in olden times. The other day we came across some silver coins of Athens, which had been found in some sands exposed by the river Oxus. It is quite possible that these coins had been in the pockets of the soldiers of Alexander the Great on the occasion of their expedition in that direction. Some time ago we met with a coin of Nero in a Punjab bazaar. How had that coin come there ? Had it come in trade ? Did one of the disciples of Paul bring it to India ?

The interest in coins is a natural one. We all toil for coins. We all spend them. We all curse the ever-lowering price of one of them. Hence it is only natural that we should be interested in the coins of other days and other countries. "Coins and inscriptions," says a learned author, "tell no lies." I am not quite sure about inscriptions, for I have read many grave-stones. About the coins I am quite as sure as I am about the grave-stones. One can easily sift the chaff and get out the wheat We then find that in India especially coins and inscriptions *make* history and do not simply illustrate it. They certainly help us to a large amount of geography. At the same time as the dies from which they were struck were the work of the artists of the day, the coins help us much in arriving at some idea of the art of the country at the time when the coins were struck. More than this coins have ever been a means of showing the religion of their strikers; so that there is something of permanent interest in the study of numismatics. I have just been reading the life of Sir Herbert Edwardes by his wife, a noble book about a great and good man. In it is a letter in which Maharaja Gulab Singh of Jammu and Kashmir is fully described. He is not spared. It seems strange after reading Sir Herbert's letter on turning to the coins of Gulab Singh to see that he caused to be put on them the Christian letters I. H. S. If we care to search out his reason for using these letters on his coins, another phase in the character of that wily ruler will be shown.

Lately I was asked to make out a list of books that have been written in the last half century on the coins of Northern India. The list was not complete, but it came up to 1886. I do not suppose any library has all these. I propose therefore in a series of papers to give hints to those interested in the study of the coins of Northern India. Beginning with the earliest coins known, I propose to go briefly through the characteristics of each series of known coins. It is quite possible that what I have to say may stir up collectors and non-collectors to work, and that the result of their activity will be the discovery of coins hitherto unknown. At the same time I feel confident that what I have to bring forward will prove of some help to those who have been collecting for some time and who have met with many difficulties. I shall avoid, as far as possible, all long names and scientific terms, and remember that I am writing in India and for those dwelling in India.

II.

IN coin-collecting, as in botanising and fern-hunting, it is best to set to work with some definite plan. We must take a look at all that comes under our observation, but choose only what we want—that which we are searching for. In starting a collection if we know what we are about, we take specimens of everything that comes to hand. After each collecting journey is over we sit down and arrange our specimens. After having done this we know what we have got, and if we know our subject well we know what we have still to look for—those we have not as yet obtained. In our future excursions these are the things we shall hunt for. As in no one book we have yet read have we yet seen a full but brief account of the coins of India, we will here try and give a *resumé* of what has been discovered by those who have given themselves, or rather their leisure hours, to the study of this interesting subject.

The coins which are considered the oldest of all Indian coins are silver pieces weighing about 50 grains. They are of no fixed shapes, being as often elliptical as rectangular or quadrilateral. Almost invariably one side is covered all over with marks which must have been made by different kinds of punches. These marks are sometimes the figure of a wheel or sun, a tree, a bullock or elephant or man, or

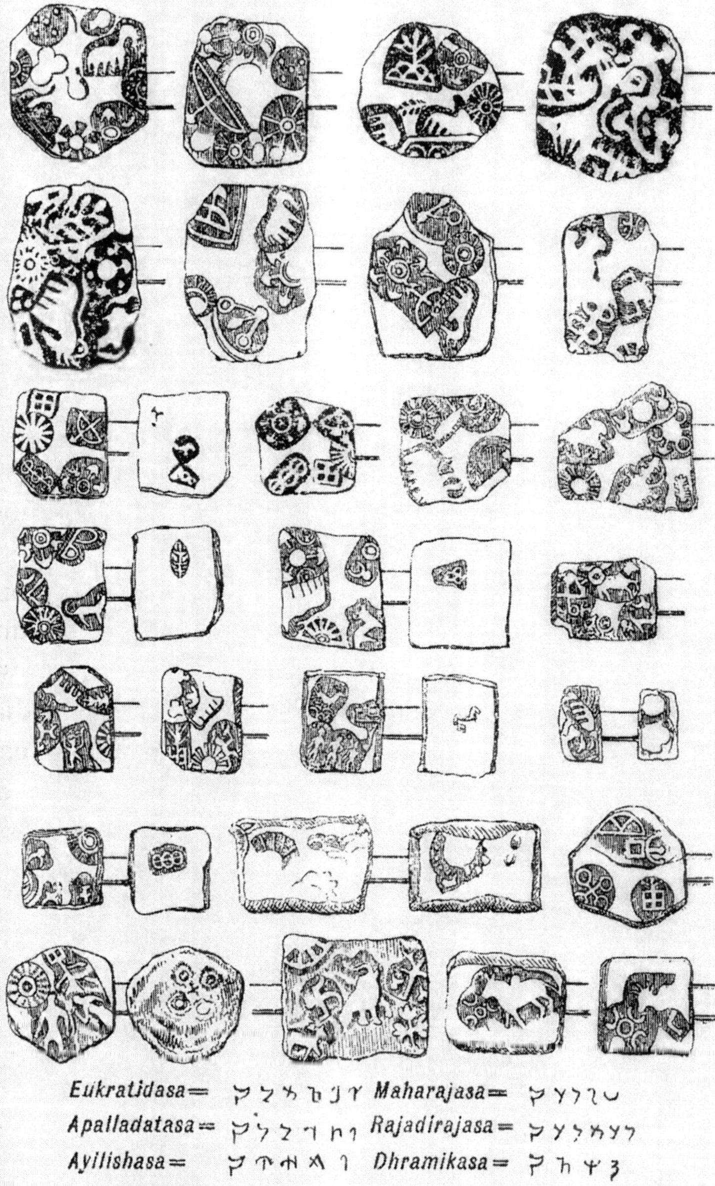

Punch marked coins and specimens of Kings' names and titles in Bactrian Pali.

a row of human figures. The other side of these coins has one or two of these punched marks. Not one has yet been found with a name or even anything approaching to a letter on it. The silver does not look pure. Nothing of this kind has as yet been found in gold. Copper coins of the same weight and with similar marks have been found, but in such small quantities that we cannot be far wrong if we say that they are imitations of the silver coins. The silver coins must have been once very numerous, judging from the numbers in which they are still found in various parts of the country. There is nothing whatever on them to indicate extraneous influence. They were probably the currency of India more than 2,000 years ago, at the time when the Greeks under Alexander the Great invaded India and before that time.

In old towns we sometimes find very small copper coins on which is a tree, round which are fragments of an inscription These may be of an age equal to the silver coins above described. In all old towns in the north of India very, very old copper coins are found. They are mostly cast and not struck. Some of them have only symbols on them, such as a deer, elephant or tree or snake or dog or lion. Sometimes they have on them a few letters, sometimes nothing but symbols. These coins are attributed to the time before the Greeks came. In the Punjab rectangular coins weighing about 180 grains are often found. They have on one side an elephant in high relief, on the other a lion. incuse, *i. e.*, struck in the inside of a lower surface. Both animals have a Buddhist symbol over them. Sometimes a horse takes the place of the lion, and over it is a star. Other rectangular coins have other devices on one side only, the other side being plain.

It would seem that all these varieties of coins were in use before the time of the Greek invasion. We know that at that time the country was divided into a great number of States. It may be that some of them were small commonwealths and not governed by a raja. Some we know were governed by rajas, however, and it may be that the letters would, if we had sufficient coins to enable us to read the whole inscription, give us their names. It is most probable that the Greeks taught the people of India to put on their coins the names of the rulers. About a hundred years after Alexander's invasion of India, Asoka ordered his edicts to be engraved on rocks, boulders and pillars. In India proper these edicts were in Indian Pali; in lands bordering on the northern confines of the country they were in Bactrian Pali. This fact shows us that we ought to expect purely Indian coins of that period to have their inscriptions in Indian Pali. Those struck in borderlands out of the influence of the Greeks would probably be in Bactrian Pali only, or might be in both Palis. Those struck in lands under Greek influence, which was felt all over the Punjab, would have the inscription on one side in Greek and on the other in Bactrian Pali, or perhaps Indian Pali. We find this was actually the case. There is a series of coins in copper struck in India in the second century before Christ. On one side there are some indistinct symbols, on the other, are in an incuse square three symbols in a row, and under the name of the king, in Indian Pali. These are called *Mitra* coins, as the word *Mitra* is with the name of the king. Again, on the border-land of Hindustan proper, *i. e.*, between the Sutlej and Jumna, coins are found in silver and copper, both sides of which are covered with symbols, round which on one side is an inscription in Indian Pali and on the other in Bactrian Pali. The coins of four kings are known which have the inscriptions in both Palis. These coins and those above mentioned are the oldest coins known in India. They show us that before the Greeks came the art of die-sinking was almost unknown, that there was no large or firm or highly-civilised Government in the land. Just as we have no buildings belonging to the ancient nations of India, we have no coins. This would seem to point out that the cities were collections of mud huts, and that commerce was carried on by barter rather than by means of any recognised medium of exchange. The absence of gold from the currency would seem to indicate the poverty of the country, or the fact that the people had not recognised it as a possible medium of exchange. Gold was not unknown to the country or in the country, for part of the revenue of Darius was derived from India in gold. But the fact remains that no gold coins that we can attribute to ancient India, *i. e.*, to India before the time of Alexander's invasion, have yet been found. The copper and silver coins we have mentioned are never found in great quantities, so it would seem they were only current in towns where constant barter would be almost an impossibility. In support of this statement we find that these coins are found only in certain localities near some old capital, and that the symbols vary as do the sites on which the coins are found. This would suggest that in those ancient days there was little intercourse between the distant parts of the Empire. Had that intercourse existed the coins of one capital could have been found in the ruins of another. Of course it may happen, and often does happen, that old coins from one part of India are found in the bazaars of other and those remote parts. This is owing to modern facilities of travelling. In exhuming old sites each one is seen to possess coins peculiar to itself if they are old.

It may be as well to mention that the two Palis are written in quite distinct characters: Indian Pali reads like English and Sanskrit from left to right, while Bactrian Pali reads from right to left, like Arabic and Persian. Modern Sanskrit letters are the outcome of Indian Pali. Bactrian Pali has ceased to be cultivated at all. Its compound letters are numerous and puzzling, but as the number of kings who used it is less than sixty, it is not difficult to master sufficient for the deciphering of coins.

A hint about collecting these old Indian coins. They are found in the generality of Indian bazaars, only in towns or large villages near old sites. As round about Delhi there are some of the oldest sites in India, in the bazaar of that old capital are the coins of many long-since-forgotten rulers. It may be as well to add another hint which will be useful at all times. When going coin-collecting, never, unless you want to pay enormously for what you purchase, go in a carriage, or in good clothes, or with servants with you, or with dalals or native brokers. Take your travelling bag and your rupees. Put on any old hat and clothes, and a sweet and taking smile, and have on your tongue some all-powerful and appropriate flattery ; keep your eyes open for the heaps of cowries and the piles of pice. Never betray your appreciation of things put before you. Regard good and bad with unconcern. Never be eager about anything put into your hand. I have noticed coin-hunters who, on beholding a rare specimen, trembled with joy as they beheld it. Now to the money-changer coins are only bullion. If he can lay hold of any clue to your anxiety to possess one of his treasures, of course he will put on a high price ; so control yourself altogether, for while you are looking at the coins, rest assured you are being most carefully watched. Don't be afraid if you are asked fabulous prices for things. You won't get old coins at bullion rates, but you may get them for their double intrinsic value, which is cheap. If you find that the money-changer is slow in selling, leave him with utter indifference, giving as you go your bag a good shake. The music of the rupee is very powerful and opens hearts and bags. It will probably cause the display of many hidden treasures. But use it not lavishly ; only as you are vanishing from the baniya's view.

It is astonishing how the silver voice when going round a corner seems to possess peculiar attractions to the squatting shopkeeper. When you have secured your treasures, value them properly. They are getting fewer and fewer every year, for coin-hunting is now-a-days a rage with many men who wish to occupy odd hours with adding to their knowledge and to the interest they wish to cultivate in this "gorgeous East" where our lot is cast, and where there seem to be so few objects of real interest.

My next paper will be an attempt to give the reader some idea about the Greek coins found in India.

III.

LEXANDER'S conquest of India was no mere raid. It was a conquest based on scientific principles. He kept up communications always with Greece. The countries he conquered he organised before he pushed his armies further. Before he came to the Punjab he had thoroughly subdued and reduced to order, and put under a firm government, not only Persia, but also the whole of Northern Afghanistan. When, therefore, he withdrew from the Punjab by way of the Indus, that part of his army might return by sea and part by land to Babylon, he left the Punjab and Kabul under rulers who governed the country. Under them the whole of the north of the Punjab, all Northern Afghanistan and South Turkistan became Hellenised. When Alexander died his Empire had not had time to become consolidated. Besides this he left no grown-up heir to succeed him. Hence his Empire split up into several immense kingdoms, which were nearly always at war with each other. It is not surprising, therefore, if the provinces on the far-off confines towards the East became the seat of dissensions. We know that Seleukus had dealings with Indian magnates, and after that the whole history of the easternmost provinces of Alexander's Empire is lost, or nearly so.

Stray notices of a Theodotus, an Apollodotus and a Menander are met with, but the history of this part has disappeared. So much of it as has been exhumed is due entirely to coins. Before we conquered the Punjab we had also dealings with Kabul. Sir Alexander Burnes, as traveller and ambassador, went there. Charles Masson resided there. The former, at the end of his books of travel, gives some plates of old coins he had met with. The latter took up the subject and collected over sixty thousand in gold, silver, and copper. All these were from Afghanistan and its old mounds and topes and ruins. Up to that time the Punjab was almost as little known as was Kabul. When, however, it came into our hands, after the Sutlej campaign and the second Punjab war, the hidden wealth of the bazaars was gradually disclosed. When the Punjab settled down to works of peace, when new roads were made, new wells dug, and old ones cleaned out, when new houses were built on old ruins, and old mounds were ransacked for building materials, when the plough of the husbandman penetrated new soil, or soil for many centuries uncultivated, when railways began to be constructed and canals dug, then it was that a constant stream of old coins set in towards the bazaars. And now there is not a town of any size or commercial importance whose bazaars have not money-changers, in whose possession are old coins going back to those times when Greek kings or satraps ruled the land of the five rivers.

The researches of numismatists have brought to light the names of over thirty Greek kings, and of three queens, who ruled either in the Punjab or in Kabul after Alexander's death. Further search may bring to light the names of other kings, for as yet the subject has not been taken up warmly. No mounds have been excavated in the Punjab, although the country is full of them, and it is known that the mounds are the covered-up ruins of old cities. However, thirty kings, new to history, make a somewhat remarkable discovery. Besides the names of the kings the coins gave us the key to a language altogether forgotten and unknown—*Bactrian Pali*. On one side of the coins are the names and titles of the king in Greek: on the other side are the same names and titles in Bactrian Pali. The same method which was used in making the Rosetta stone give up the key to the hieroglyphics of Egypt, made the Greek of the coins useful in deciphering Bactrian Pali. The clue being obtained, was followed up, and in a few years the coins Masson had discovered were read and identified. By the help thus obtained the inscriptions of Asoka at Shabbazgurhi and Mansehra have been read, written as they are in Bactrian Pali. There are some few other inscriptions in the same character, and they, too, have been mastered. These two discoveries have placed Indian numismatics in a light very different from the coin-lore of other countries. They show distinctly that Indian coins do not only help to illustrate history; they help us to make it, as well as to illustrate it. Let me take by way of showing what I mean by coins illustrating history—a very simple case. Just lately there have been found some coins of Nasr, son of Nasir-ud-din,

These tell us that they were struck in Sijistan, the country west of Kandahar, in the year 400 Hijri, *i. e.*, about 900 years ago, in the reign of Mahmud of Ghazni, the great conqueror of India. Turning to the History of Mahmud, who was also son of Nasir-ud-din Subaktagin, we find he had a brother who ruled over Sijistan and with whom he lived in peace. It seems strange that no coins of Nasr should have been found till this year. I say they serve to illustrate and confirm history. They do not tell us much that is new, but they illustrate what historians had recorded. If, however, we dip into our list of Greek kings and take up a coin, we find it has on one side the helmeted head or bare head of a queen named Agathokleia, and that the other side contains the name of her husband Straton. That he was her husband is confirmed by another coin, on one side of which are the busts of both, side by side, as in our coins of William and Mary. These coins we say make history. Till they were discovered we did not know that a part of India was once governed conjointly by a queen and king. The queen occupying the place of honour on the coin, it is conjectured that she was ruler by right. Here is a hint, or more, ground-work for a historical novel.

We call these coins Græco-Bactrian because of their having the two languages on them, and because the Greek kingdom of Theodotus, or Diodotus as it is on the coins, was in Bactria or Turkistan. As a list of the kings' names hitherto discovered has never yet been published, the names of the kings found on

Plate II

Græco - Bactrian and Indo - Scythian Coins.

coins obtained in the Punjab is here given. They are Alexander, Seleukus, Lysimachus, Antiochus Sophytes, Diodotus, Eythydemus I., Demetrius, Eythydemus II., Pantaleon, Agathokles, Antimachus Theos, Eukratides, Heliokles, Antialkidas, Lysias, Diomedes, Archebius, Apollodotus, Strato, *Agathokleia*, Menander, Epander, Dionysius, Zoilus, Apollophanes, Artemidorus, Antimachus Nikephoros, Philoxenes, Nikias, Hippostratus, Amyntas, Hermæus, *Kalliope*, Telephus, Plato, Theophilus, Peukalaus, *Laodike*. Those in *italics* are queens. Here is a list of names and work for the historian. As yet, however, no systematic and scientific investigation has taken place in the mounds of the Punjab, and we are without the aid of inscriptions, for no Greek inscription has yet been found. Now as all these coins are in Greek on one side and in either Bactrian Pali or Indian Pali on the other, after the time of Demetrius, it is almost a certain thing that they left behind them diglo inscriptions. Hitherto, however, archæological research has been so fitful a thing and so one-sided, having been chiefly made with respect to the illustration of Buddhism, that many of the oldest sites in the Punjab have been left untouched. Scholarly men have ruled in the Punjab, and our Governors-General have also been literary men of no mean standing, but still the antiquities of the Punjab have been only partially explored. Last year, indeed, the Archæological Survey was closed in the Punjab owing to the most gross misrepresentations of work accomplished there. The history of all these kings, therefore, except Alexander, as far as the Punjab is concerned, has to be worked out.

The coins of these kings are worthy of study. Some are in copper only, and in that metal coins are as often square as round. The silver coins are oboli (small silver coins) hemidrachmas, drachmas, didrachmas and tetradrachmas. The coins of Diodotus and Eythydemus only have been found in gold. The obverse or right side of the coin has often on it the bust of the king or queen. Sometimes this bust is covered with a helmet, sometimes it has only the fillet or diadem. Here we are then face to face with these kings. We have their portraits and can see what they were like. We have their titles,—the Saviour, the Righteous, the Unconquered, the Victorious, the Father-lover, the Good-worker. The reverse or other side of the coin generally has the figure of a god of Greece on it, with the inscription in Pali, the translation of the Greek. There are Jupiter, Hercules, Apollo, Pallas, Nike, Poseidon, the Dioscuri, &c. There are also purely Indian devices,—the elephant, the Indian bull, &c. All this is material for history and food for the philosopher. In the execution of the coins we notice a gradual decadence. Many of the coins are in such exquisite condition, they look as if they must have been fresh from the mint when they were put on one side. Many again have seen much service and are worn, but still the images and devices are legible. Most of the coins have monograms on them. What these monograms mean we do not know. Some may be dates. Others, however, cannot be so, and it has been conjectured they are the names of the mint towns, or it may be mint masters. The opinions of the learned differ on this matter. When we remember that in the history of India our knowledge of this period, previous to the discovery of these coins, was *nil*, we see how exceedingly helpful coins may be in filling up some of the gaps in the story of the Empire. We have seen that much has yet to be done. Every collection of coins, however, helps to confirm and extend our knowledge. The reader shall see in the next chapter that further aid may be expected from coins in working out the history of India about the time that our era began. We shall see also what a pressing need there is for inscriptions, which often give genealogies. We are left very much to conjecture with respect to the relationship of the kings whose names we have given, and we know almost nothing of their actions.

IV.

HITHERTO the names of the kings which have been in Greek on the coins have been Greek names. The names on the other sides of the same coins have been the same Greek names transliterated into Pali. But if we examine a series of coins bearing the name of Hermæus in Greek, we find on the other side the name of a new king with a new title—*Kujula Kadphises, king of the Kushans.* The king's head is not the same on these coins as it is on the ordinary coins of Hermæus. There is a lot of coins with the same kind of head, however, but these have the name *Kadphises* on in Greek. On the Pali side the inscription remains the same. So the inference is that Kadphises reigned along with Hermæus for some time and at last succeeded him. There is another Kadphises whose coins are very abundant; he is called *Hima* or *Wemo* Kadphises. The coins of the later Greek kings were all in silver and copper. The coins of Hima Kadphises are in gold and copper only, none being known of silver. The king is represented on these gold and copper coins as wearing a Tatar head-dress and coat, Tatar trousers and Tatar boots. On the other side is a humped bull. Left therefore to the coins, we infer that he came from Tatary, from which it is probable he brought large quantities of gold, that he conquered India, and made that country his home. The coins of three other kings are also in gold and copper, but unlike the coins of the two kings bearing the name of Kadphises, which have the names on one side in Greek and on the other their transliteration, these have the name of the king in Greek on one side and on the reverse the name and image of some god, which is sometimes Greek, sometimes Persian, and sometimes Indian, but which has at all times the name in Greek letters, which have been adapted to represent certain Indian sounds. These three kings are Kenerki or Kanishka, Overki or Huvishka, and Bazdeo or Vasu Deva. Both in gold and copper the coins of these three kings are exceedingly numerous. The copper coins seem to have been the type on which the kings of India went on striking for many years if not centuries. The degradation of the images keeps pace with that of the Greek : at last the letters disappear, and only an attempt at the representation of an image is left on either side. It is hard work to guess what the image is intended to represent.

An old history of Kashmir tells us that these three kings reigned over that country at the same time, and that they were of Turashka origin and by profession Buddhists. The coins, however, tell another tale somewhat. The kings reigned over Kashmir, having conquered it. They reigned, however, one after the other, and even in their time the decadence in Greek art and literature was marked. The coins of Kanishka are often really good. The coins of Huvishka, however, are of a decidedly lower stamp. The coins of Vasu Deva are sometimes illegible. Although the historian of Kashmir claims these three kings for the country, very few of their coins are found in the valley, but in every old mound of the Punjab these coins abound. The names of these five kings are not Greek. They are probably Scythian, and because they reigned and coined in India we call them Indo-Scythian kings.

But older than these five-king coins is a very large series on which occur many names, which are not of Greek origin, though written in Greek letters. These coins are in silver and copper, not one having yet been obtained in gold. The names occurring on them are Mayes, Azes, Vonones, Spalyrises, Spalahores, Spalagadames, Gondopharres, Abdagases, Sasan, Orthagnes, Pakores, Azilises, Sanabares, Arsakes, Aspa Varma, Zeionises, Rajubula, Spaleizes, and one king without a name who rejoices in the title of "*The Great Saviour, the King of Kings.*"

The coins of Mayes, both silver and copper, are round and square. The images on them are of many different kinds ; the sizes and weights show that the coins were well adapted for the exigencies of trade. The Greek inscriptions are translated into Pali just as in the Græco-Bactrian series. The execution is quite as good as that of the coins of some of the later ones of that series. Hence it has been inferred that Mayes reigned in the Punjab at the same time as these later kings. That he reigned a long time is pretty certain from the number of his coins and from the varieties of their types. Azes and Azilises would seem to come next, and in all probability they were brothers, for coins are known which have one name on one side and the other name on the reverse. Indeed, not only Azes and Azilises seem to have been related, but Vonones, Spalahores, Spalyrises and Spalagadames all seem to have been related one to the other, as well as to Azes. Not many of the coins of Vonones are found in the Punjab, but the coins of Azes are very common, both in silver and copper. No square silver coin of Azes is known, but his square copper ones are numerous. The images are of many kinds on both the silver and copper coins; the commonest is perhaps that of the king on horseback with a spear at rest or a whip in his hand. The reverses have often either Jupiter or Pallas in various attitudes. On the copper coins are the horse, the humped bull, the camel, the yak, the lion, elephant, &c.

The coins of Azilises are again very numerous both in silver and copper, and their workmanship is quite equal to that of the coins of Mayes and Azes. On them, however, there is no rèlationship stated to Azes, although their names come occasionally on the same coin. Some of the varieties in silver are very rare. The images are similar to those on the coins of Mayes and Azes. The workmanship and types of the coins of these seven kings place them in a group by themselves. The names of the kings are Scythian; but as most of the coins are found in the Punjab, except those of Vonones, it follows that six of the kings reigned in that country or in parts of it.

The coins of "*The King of Kings, the Great Saviour*," are found, but only in copper, all over the Punjab, in great quantities. Who he was we don't know.

His coins give his bust on one side, sometimes with a helmet, but generally without one, and the other side is a horseman, round which is the name and title in poor Greek. His coins are known in at least six types. I have seen hundreds of the same type, but never two that were from the same die. This reveals a fact to us that is somewhat startling—there were in the Punjab die-sinkers who could produce dies in which were cut Greek images and Greek letters? These men must have been numerous and capable of turning out a number of dies annually. This fact is further attested by the varieties of the coins of the other Scythian kings. The workmanship was not fine, but it was passable. As these Scythian kings must have reigned about the time of Christ, we have the fact that Grecian art had not died out of the Punjab 330 years after Alexander's invasion.

There is one coin of Azes which is worthy of a separate notice. It has on its reverse instead of the translation of the name and titles of the king, this inscription : "The son of Indra Varma, Aspa Varma, the Strategic and Victorious." Here we have an Indian name, Aspa Varma. He was probably a general of Azes—a man who must have studied the tactics of Greek warfare successfully, for he is called Strategic, and as a result of his skill in strategy—Victorious. He was not a Scythian, but a son of the soil. So we find that it was the policy of Azes, as of Akbar and of our own Government, to use the brave soldiers of India for conquering and ruling their own land. This coin shows that Azes must have been constantly engaged in war, and that his own Scythian officers had either been killed or superseded. Aspa Varma is the only general whose name occurs on the Indo-Scythian series. That this coin was not a medal is seen from its weight and from the numbers in which it occurs. Most bazaars in the Punjab yield some specimens.

There is another group of coins belonging to men with Scythian names. These coins are poorer in execution than any of those previously described. They are all in copper. The most common type has a head on one side and an image of a winged Victory on the other. Round the head is the name in very poor Greek, and on the reverse its translation in Pali. There are other types, all much worn and very poor, showing that they have enjoyed extensive circulation. The name of the king is Gondopharres. His nephew was Abdagases. A relative of his was Sasan and another relative was Orthagnes. Others who were probably related to Gondopharres were Sanabares and Pakores.

There is a singular interest attaching to these coins, and specially to those of Gondopharres. From a study of the coins themselves it was inferred that they were struck about 40 or 50 *A. D.* Now in a book of legends it is stated that Thomas the Apostle came to India and was murdered by a king named Gudapharasa. The presence of Roman gold coins of Roman emperors in the topes of Jalalabad and the Punjab shows that trade existed between Northern India and Europe about the time of the Christian era. This trade most likely came by the way of Persia and Northern Afghanistan. What so probable then as that Thomas, in obedience to the Saviour's last parting words, should come to India by that route? The coins of Gondopharres are found in the Northern Punjab, but there is one type which seems to be found only near Kandahar. They are very numerous, and this argues that Gondopharres reigned a long time. If the king of this name who reigned in Kandahar is the same as the one who reigned in the Peshawar valley, his kingdom was extensive. If this be the king who murdered Thomas, then later traditions which make his place of martyrdom near Madras must be altered. Here we have a group of coins, with not only a family likeness, but with a monogram of unvarying form on the coins of the different kings, all telling us something about the king who murdered an Apostle of Jesus Christ. The coins belong to the Punjab and its vicinity. Such coins must be not only to the Christian but to the historian of India of surpassing interest. Kadphises and his series, Mayes and Vonones and their family, are of interest because they help us in the history of the Punjab. Gondopharres, however, came in touch with Christianity, and his actions probably influenced India in such a way as to involve its history in a darkness not yet dispelled. Had Thomas influenced India as Paul did Rome, what might not have happened?

We have not yet done with these Indo-Scythian coins. There are silver coins, didrachmas, on which is found the name of Zeionises, a satrap. The reverse gives us something additional; it tells us that Zeionises satrap was son of satrap Manigul. There are copper coins of two sizes which confirm this story.

Other coins reveal the names of other satraps, such as Rajubula and Kharamostis and Saudasa. We may see from the style of these coins that they belong to the Indo-Scythian group. The figures on them and the style of the writing are debased, as we might expect to see on coins struck in outlying Provinces, over which it was necessary to appoint governors so nearly independent that they struck coins in their own names, omitting the name of the king, but adding to their own names the title of subordination—satrap. Such kings must have been in reality independent. These satrap coins, however, give us an idea about the extent of country subjugated by the Indo-Scythians and afterwards governed by them.

In all probability there are coins to be discovered which will reveal more names than those already known to us. There are many mounds in the Punjab whose secrets have not been revealed because they have not as yet been excavated. When the Government shall have some repose from frontier petty wars and vexations, when the country shall have peace, and the railways and canals bring prosperity and begin to yield some interest on the millions spent on their construction, then perhaps the attention of Government will be paid to the antiquities of the Punjab—antiquities which will be all the more valuable from the money spent on their being brought to light. In the coins we have in our museums and collections, however, we have sufficient to show us that the Indo-Scythian coins of India are a group worthy of being assiduously collected and carefully studied, for they belong to those coins which make history.

V.

BEFORE leaving the coins with Greek letters on them found in the Punjab and Northern India, we ought perhaps to refer to coins which were not struck in India or near it, but which still have found their way into the country, and which are occasionally met with in the bazaars.

After Alexander's death the kingdom of Syria was ruled by a series of kings, most of whom had the name of Antiochus. Thirteen kings of that name ruled there and six with the name Seleukus. The silver coins of these men are sometimes obtained in Karachi and Bombay. As each Antiochus had his own special and additional title, we cannot go into this matter here, but only say that the style of the coins is quite different to that of the Græco-Bactrian coins, and that it requires a separate study.

In Parthia, about the middle of the third century before Christ, Arsakes I. established an empire which lasted till about the middle of the third century *A. D.* About thirty kings reigned in 500 years, and the coins of these kings found their way to India. They can easily be identified. One side has the head of the king and the other has a man seated holding an arrow, and round him are the name and titles of the king in Greek. As, however, all these thirty kings had the name Arsakes, the assignment of each coin to the king who struck it is a most difficult matter, even for a British Museum expert. These Parthian coins exhibit the same deterioration in art mentioned above in connection with the Græco-Bactrian and Indo-Scythian series. The portraits of the early kings are portraits; those of the later are caricatures. There are books on both the Syrian and Parthian coins, and to those we must refer our readers who intend taking up the study of the coins of those kings.

Rome was in her glory for the two centuries before and after Christ. As we have not yet got beyond that period we may stay to inquire after the Roman coins found in India. As yet there has been no great find of Roman coins in the Punjab. Some old topes in Afghanistan yielded gold coins of Domitian, Trajan and Hadrian, and as we know when these kings lived, we know that the buildings in which their coins were found must have been erected after their time. Here we have an example of known coins helping us to a history before unknown—the history of a certain class of buildings.

In the south of India, however, gold and silver Roman coins have often been found in the most perfect state of preservation. The records of the Madras Museum tell us about the dates of "*the finds*" and their contents. That Museum has in its cabinets 76 Roman coins, about half of which are gold, but since the catalogue was printed the learned curator, Dr. Thurston, has reported the discovery of a further find of Roman gold coins; and Dr. Hultzsch states that a large find of silver coins has lately taken place in Mysore, and that the Mysore Government has secured a good quantity of them. Thus it would appear that in the early centuries of the Christian era the flow of gold must have set in from the west towards the east, and the flow still continues without any sign of reflux. Should anyone wish to identify any Roman coin he may find in the north or south of India,—is there not a dictionary of Roman coins by S. M. Stevenson—a manual of 929 pages of double columns? The subject of the coins of the Roman empire is a vast one, and only a student of many years can give information worthy of credit about a coin. As a rule, however, the emperor's name is on the coin and is legible. The other day we found a lovely coin of Nero in a North Indian bazaar, and we have seen gold and silver coins of several Roman emperors.

It will be as well here to state that the greatest care must be taken with respect to the genuineness of all the coins of which we have hitherto spoken. The desire to possess Græco-Bactrian coins, with Greek inscriptions on one side and its translation into Pali on the other, was so great that high prices began to be paid shortly after their discovery was made known. For the last fifty years those prices have been steadily going up. One hundred and twenty pounds was given in one instance for one single silver coin!! The dealers keep a book in which an impression is entered of every coin they purchase and part with. Should a coin turn up from an old mound, and its images and inscriptions not correspond with any of the impressions preserved in their book, they at once put down its price at a fabulous sum. We have seen Rs. 2,000, Rs. 700, Rs. 500, Rs. 250 asked for single silver coins. Copper coins of great rarity and beauty often fetch twenty rupees.

No wonder the coin-dealers could not resist turning a dishonest penny. The temptation was great. Not only were impressions on paper preserved, but also each coin had a mould made from it. Carefully and slowly results of these moulds were put forward. No unique coin has been discovered in the Punjab, of which, in a few years, copies or casts were not presented for sale by the dealers. These copies are not only of gold and silver but of copper coins. Fortunately coin-dealers are not artists or even artistic. The moulds they take are not perfect. There are points in a real Greek coin which cannot be obtained correct and sharp from casting in a mould. These are the ear, the eyes and eyeball, the nostrils, the lips and mouth. Should the mould break and an attempt be made by an artist the result needs not to be criticised. Lately, however, great progress has been made in the imitation of Græco-Bactrian coins. An artistic element has been introduced. New dies have been made or new moulds, but still the original Greek artistic finish has not been attained. Besides this, not only must the artist finish off the images, he must give the inscriptions correctly. The artist who has often done well in the former "comes a cropper" when he attempts the latter. Hence to guard one's self from being cheated it is wise to seek aid from an expert or from books before purchasing expensive coins. Dealers boldly demand hundreds of rupees for coins they know are copies. They will give you a history to each piece : how this was dug up on the banks of the Amu, this in Swat, this in Belgram, this in Hazara, this in Manikyala, and they will tell you the village where they purchased each coin. Verily all men are liars, and especially Indian coin-dealers. We have found the best way is to wait and have nothing to do with them.

We do not know exactly when the Indo-Scythian kings ceased to reign or when they stopped coining. But we know that in the fourth century of our era coins were struck by a king whose family name was Gupta. These Gupta coins are mostly in gold, though some are also in silver and some, fewer and rarer still, in copper. We must not confound these Gupta coins with Chandra Gupta or Sandracottus, who was king of Magadha in the time of Alexander and Seleukus, three hundred years before Christ. The Gupta coins are out-and-out Indian. They exhibit but faint traces of Grecian influence. Both sides have figures on them and inscriptions in Sanskrit. The art is Indian, the subjects Indian, the execution Indian. One female figure seated on a lion, or a throne with a cornucopia on her left shoulder, seems to remind us somewhat of some of the Indo-Scythian gold coins. One peculiarity of the coins is the name of the king. It is generally written downwards, one letter *below* the other. (Does this show that some extraneous influence was at work ? Chinese ?) The figures on the coins are generally the king and queen, or king only on one side. On the other is a female—a goddess. The king generally has a bow in his hand; in some instances he is slaying a lion; in others he has his son with him. Sometimes he is on horseback: sometimes there is the horse alone. In nearly all cases the king is accompanied by the bird-standard. In one case he is playing a musical instrument.

The kings of this dynasty, whose coins are known, are Chandra Gupta I. and his wife Kumara Devi, Samudra Gupta, Chandra Gupta II., Kumara Gupta and Skanda Gupta; but the names of Nara Baladitya, Prakasaditya, and Kramaditya are also found on coins similar in type and style.

Much of late has been done with respect to these Gupta kings. Mr. J. F. Fleet has worked out the inscriptions of these kings. Mr. V. A. Smith, *C. S.*, has written exhaustively on the coins, describing every known specimen. Mr. E. J. Rapson, of the British Museum Coin Department, has written on the Gupta coins in the Bodleian collection. Dr. Hoernle has given us an account of a large copper-silver seal of Kumara Gupta, on which is given the genealogy of the Gupta family. When all these results are put together it will be seen how useful the labours of the epigraphist and numismatist and archæologist are, and how they combine to produce trustworthy history. Unfortunately for us the coins of the Guptas are few. In India our museums have scarcely any. In no case has any collector ever managed to get a hundred together. Now-a-days they are scarcely ever found. Fifty years ago they were not numerous. The silver coins are very small, only about the size of a two-anna piece. They have a head on one side and a Sanskrit legend on the other, going round an object which is perhaps intended for a peacock. The copper coins have generally a head on one side or half-size portrait of a man, and a bird with outstretched wings on the other. These coins are scarcely known in the Punjab, but are found south of the Sutlej and as far east as Patna. Most of those hitherto obtained have been taken out of the country. There are, however, we believe two or perhaps three private collections of these coins still in India. The great age of these coins, the evidence of inscriptions, and the fact that they are purely Indian coins, or nearly so, go far to create a deep interest in them. To the student of Indian history they are simply engrossing in their interest. No one with Gupta materials before him can say that the study of Indian history is dull.

We do not know exactly where these Gupta kings reigned and coined. It was probably somewhere in the North-West Provinces or North-Western Bengal. Their influence was widespread and extended westwards as far as Gujerat. These coins with the Gupta inscriptions give us the history to some extent of about two centuries. We want, however, more coins and better specimens, and specially we need that our Indian museums should secure for the Indian students of Indian history at any rate typical sets of the coins of these old Indian kings.

VI.

THE chronology of the Guptas having been fixed, we are not quite so much at a loss in assigning several series of coins to a certain time. Every student of Indian inscriptions sees at a glance that the style of the letters is a pretty sure guide to the age when they were written. There is a small mound called Sunet, three miles west of Ludhiana, on which small square copper coins have been found. They have a wheel on one side and a name, without any titles, on the other. Along with these coins are found baked impressions of seals in clay and also baked impressions of coins. The letters of all three kinds of objects are similar in style—that of the Gupta inscription and of the Gupta coins. Hence it is inferred that Sunet was in its glory when Gupta kings were reigning. It is not a large place, but, according to tradition, it had its rajas. The small copper coins give several names, probably those of the rajas of Sunet. They were not a rich people, and their coins were small and only in copper. East of Umballa were several old towns. In the bazaars of Sadhaura and Jagadhari a series of coins has been found, covered with Buddhist emblems on one side, and having on the other the figure of a man with six heads, and an inscription in Gupta letters. So we may judge that fifteen hundred years ago the plains below Sirmoor had their rajas who enjoyed the privilege of coining. There seems to have been no paramount sovereign of Northern India at that time. The country seems to have been divided into a host of small rajaships.

We know, however, that Kashmir had a long line of rulers. The history of Kashmir tries to make us believe that some of these rulers conquered India. If so, they must have been soon expelled. There are, however, undoubtedly coins of Miharkal found in the Punjab. They have on one side a man's head with the name Miharkal in front of it: the other side has a bull on it and a Sanskrit inscription. Now, Miharkal is said to have invaded Lanka or Ceylon. There are other coins somewhat similar in size and weight to the coins of Miharkal, but with a wheel on them and only a few letters—"*To*," which are perhaps the first letters of Toramana, another great soldier of Kashmir. If, however, we take up a translation of the history of Kashmir we find it had many kings of whom no coins have as yet been found.

There is a series of coins found in the Punjab about which many writers have been severely exercised. On one side is an armless, headless figure, which may be a fish, or a piece of machinery, or an altar, but which on really good specimens resolves itself into something like a human figure, the head being represented by a ball and the neck not being represented at all. The other side of the coin has a figure clothed in what seems at first something like

Plate III.

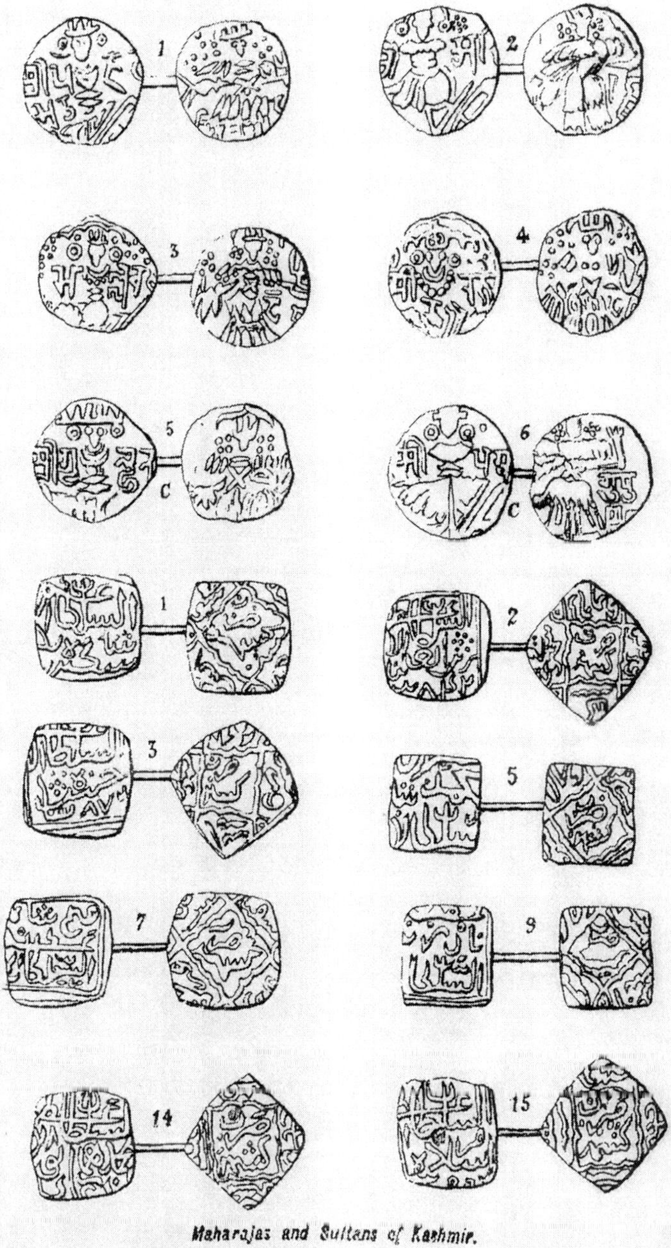

Maharajas and Sultans of Kashmir.

a night shirt, but which study shows to be a coat of mail. The natives everywhere call them the coins of Raja Sarkat or Sarkap, of folklore notoriety. But fortunately, along with the usually headless trunk the coins give names, which are certainly those of old rajas of Kashmir, such as Durlabha, Pratapa, Vinaya and others. As these coins abound, but are always in bad condition, it is probable that some day the names of other rajas will be discovered. There is one peculiarity about these Sarkap coins : they are a compound of gold, silver, and copper. As in no two known coins do the proportions of these metals seem the same, it is difficult to see how they could have ever been a medium of exchange. As we get further on we shall have to refer again to this matter in connection with an extensive series of coins.

As we have touched on the matter of the old coins of Kashmir it may be as well to go on with them. About a thousand years ago the coins of Kashmir got into a groove which they kept in for about 400 years. On one side of the coin was a seated male figure with ear-rings, the posture was stiff in the extreme. Sometimes the bare legs were shown, but at all times there was an attempt made to show the skirts which Highlanders of Kashmir and Caledonia used to love. The waist is bound round with a long rope-like girdle. On the head is an attempt, such as a child of three might make, at a king's crown. The head of the king was originally like a potato with eyes in it, but that in later specimens was altered for three circles, the uppermost two of which were intended for eyes and the lower one for mouth, nose, and chin. Round the neck was a band of solid gold, below which was suspended a necklace of fine beads. On the other side was a standing figure, which was also crowned, but the ear-rings were replaced by *ear-drops*. A cross-band bound the waist. The legs were enveloped in divided skirts, each side being doubled, *i. e.*, consisting of upper and lower parts. The left hand held a flower, the right seemed engaged in making an offering. The figure with ear-rings is that of a male, the one with ear-drops that of a female. The names in these coins are in Sanskrit letters. One or two letters are on the left side of the male figure, where his arm should be; on the right side are other letters. Turning the coin over, under the left arm of the female figure are other letters. If we join the letters together, we may get a complete name, but as a rule several letters have to be inserted, as the die of the coin was evidently larger than the piece of metal struck. The coins of about twenty-five of these Kashmir rajas are known, but, strange to say, the inhabitants of the earthly Paradise of to-day know nothing whatever about them beyond the fact that they are "*purane paise*," and that some Englishmen are such fools that they sometimes give four annas for one. The rajas of Kashmir ceased to reign about 600 years ago. For a thousand years before that time the art of die-sinking seems to have been at a standstill. No progress whatever was made, and deterioration was impossible, for the original type was too low to admit of it.

The coins which are most common in the Punjab are of silver. They have on one side a bull, seated. Over him is a name in Sanskrit. The other side has a horseman, on either side of whose head is a letter. These coins are about the size of a four-anna piece. The names of Samanta Deva, Syalapati Deva, Bhima Deva and Khvadavayaka came on them. There are copper coins on which is an elephant on one side and a rampant lion on the other. These have over the elephant one of two names, either Samanta Deva or Vanka Deva. In every bazaar these coins are found. Every old ruin seems to yield them. In small copper the same bull and horseman are found, but no other name than Samanta Deva has yet been found on these. It would seem that some nine hundred or a thousand years ago Samanta Deva, &c., were kings of Kabul, Brahmins and kings, bull worshippers and warriors. They left their mark on the coinage of the country. Dynasty after dynasty adopted the bull and horseman, and the numismatics of about three centuries in India show how firmly the idea had obtained possession of the Indian royal mind. (We must not sneer, what about our Lion and Unicorn, and St. George and the Dragon?) No gold bull and horseman coin has yet been found. When Mahmud of Ghazni took the fort of Nagarkote or Kangra, the coins in silver which he obtained there were most likely the coins of three Brahmin kings of Kabul. It is just possible that these kings were Punjab sovereigns who ruled over Kabul, and not Kabul kings who ruled over the Punjab. One thing is certain, the maharajas of the most ancient line of sovereigns in the whole Punjab, the maharajas of Trigarta or Jalandhar, whose capital was Kangra, adopted the style of these coins. The Kangra series is one, however, peculiar to itself. The coins in diameter are only about the size of a two-anna piece, but they are as thick as a half-anna piece. The horseman is never all there, portions of both horse and rider are always missing: the parts unmistakable are the spear and the thigh of the rider. It takes years of study to find out any portion of the horse or anything further of the rider. The bull is intended to be represented. The hump and the rump go a long way. The rest have to be imagined. Sometimes the name of the ruler occupies the space over the bull, sometimes the whole side of a coin. From one coin both horseman and bull disappear; the raja's name takes up one side, the name of the deity he worshipped the other. As the names of the rajas are in Hill Sanskrit, and as the names and titles are never on in full, there is nothing more puzzling at first in Indian numismatics than these coins of the old rulers of Kangra.

In following these old Indian coins we have, however, skipped two series which are of the greatest importance, the coins of the Sassanian kings of Persia and those of the caliphs or khalifas. The Sassanians were fire worshippers. Their coins had on one side a bust of the king, and on the other a fire altar, with, sometimes, attendants. These coins were in gold, silver, and copper. The gold were substantial coins, the silver and copper nearly always thin. On the earliest coins the heads of the kings are most elaborately executed, but as time went on deterioration set in and ran its course. The inscriptions on these coins are in Pahlavi, the ancient language of the Parsis and of their religious books. It is one extremely difficult to read, and the changes which took place in it do not make the difficulty less. The head-dresses of the kings and their crowns are most elaborate, and as each king had his own distinctive style the study of the coins is rendered most interesting. When the Sassanian kings had been conquered by the Musalmans, then we find in the margins Arabic inscriptions, which are amongst the earliest stamped Arabic legends in existence. These Sassanian coins are often found in the Punjab and Bombay. To the Parsis of modern India they are of the deepest interest. To us who now hold India, and who are students of the old religions and of all the histories of the world, they are of equal interest. They carry us back to a people who worshipped God under the sign of fire, but who were as laborious then as they are now. No one can read Haug's Essays on the Parsis and not rise from the book without this idea, that the Parsis had got firmly hold of the idea that to toil was the highest end of man and that labour constituted nobility.

The coins of the khalifas are too big a subject to begin at the end of a paper. They must have one to themselves.

VII.

FROM the time of the earliest coinage of the world to that of Mahomed, about twelve centuries had passed away. During that period Greece and all countries included in the world speaking and using the Greek language, and Rome and all countries conquered by Rome, had used coinage on which were not only words but devices or images of some kind or other. Mahomedanism was a most complete and thorough revolution in politics as well as in religion. Just as the Puritans of the time of the Commonwealth destroyed all sculptured decorations in the churches of England, so the Mahomedans destroyed all the images Christians had set up in the churches of the east. Many writers think the scourge was a salutary one. The second commandment was obeyed to the very letter. Had the Musalmans been as particular about the sixth, seventh, and eighth commandments, history would have had a less highly-coloured story to relate. The four successors of Mahomed who managed affairs in Arabia,—Abu Bakr, Umr, Othman, and Ali, and Ali's sons Hasan and Hussain,—were not sovereigns. When Syria and Persia had been conquered, however, necessity arose that there should be a government. For years the seat of that government was Damascus. Ockley, in his history of the Saracens, says that coins were first struck by the 5th Amawi khalifa Abdul Malik, in the Hijri year 77 or 696-7 *A.D.* Mahomed had died in the year 632 *A. D.* So for sixty-four years after his death there was no separate Mahomedan coinage. On the coins of the Sassanians, however, in the margin some Arabic words were struck. Also on coins struck at different towns in Syria, along with the sign of the cross and other devices, were struck not only Arabic names but Arabic sentences. In all this, however, there was no departure from the style of coins current in the empires of the east. The new coinage, however, of Abdul Malik was like nothing that had appeared previously. It was of gold, silver, and copper. The gold coins were about three-quarters of an inch in diameter and weighed about 66 grains. They were called dinars. The silver coins were about an inch in diameter and weighed about 45 grains. Of the copper coins, not many have come down to us, and we may leave them out altogether, as few are found in Indian bazaars. Both silver and gold coins were covered all over on both sides with inscriptions in Arabic. In the centre of the gold coins, on one side were the words : "There is no god but God, the One, the Partnerless." Round this, without the intervention of a circle, came "Mahomed is the prophet of God, whom He sent with direction and the true faith." On the other side in the middle of the coin came "God, One God, the Eternal : He begetteth not, nor is begotten." Round this again, without a circle, was stamped : "In the name of God this dinar was struck in the year" so and so. There was little variation in these inscriptions except in the matter of the year, but the mints seem to have been at work so regularly that it is possible to obtain a coin of every year from 77 Hijri for centuries. The year was in words, not in figures. (If the Arabs had figures in those days they never used them on their coins.) The silver coins were thinner than the gold and broader. On the one side they had, *in a circle*, the same as the gold: "There is no god but God, the Partnerless." Round it with a circle also *outside it*, came : "In the name of God this dirham (drachma) was struck" in such and such a place in the year so and so. The other side had, but *in a circle*, "God, One God, the Eternal: He begetteth not, nor is begotten, and there is none equal unto Him." The circle round this being larger than the one round the gold coins, the inscription was extended to :—"Mahomed is the apostle of God, whom He sent with guidance and the true faith, that He might exalt it above all creeds, even though idolaters be adverse thereto." The silver coinage, therefore, is more valuable than the gold, as it gives us the names of the towns where each piece was struck. Amongst the silver of the Amawi khalifas we have coins struck at Balkh, Herat, and Sijistan (Siestan) and at Afreekiya (Africa) and Andalus (Spain or Andalusia). This gives some idea as to the extent of the sway of the early Musalman rulers.

When the Abbasi khalifas began to rule in Bagdad, the gate of safety or peace, as it was called, some few alterations were made in the inscriptions on the coins, *e.g.*, the names of the khalifas were introduced on the coins, and sometimes the name of the moneyer or superintendent of the mint, but the main features of the coins remained. The greater part of both sides was devoted to religious formulæ, and both sides were covered with Arabic inscriptions. There was no image or ornament on the coins. This continued for centuries. When we come to think on these gold and silver coins and their inscriptions, we are astonished that the people who prepared them did not think of something further. There must have been millions of coins struck, and each coin had on it Mahomedan teaching, and was therefore a propagandist. It never struck any one in those days that the whole Quran could be easily stamped on gold or silver: least of all did it enter any one's mind that an adaptation of the coining process might be applied to the reproduction of books. It took 700 more years for mankind to hatch that, and by that time there was no khalifa reigning in Damascus or Bagdad. I do not think the learned vicar of Swavesey, the author of the *History of the Saracens*, could have seen the silver coinage of the khalifas. He says it "was rude at first." On the contrary, numismatists tell at once by the degree of perfection of the coinage, its age. The older it is the more perfect it is found. But Simon Ockley was, like many modern Orientalists, very poor. After his death "the widow remained destitute of necessaries, incapable of assisting her children." Ockley's biographer remarks :—"*Thus* students have devoted their days to studies worthy of a student. They are public benefactors, yet find no friend in the public, who cannot appreciate their value. Ministers of State know it, though they have rarely protected them." Similar cases are known in India at the present day. The coinage of Bagdad and Damascus was imitated in Andalusia, Grenada, Valencia, Malaya and Northern Africa; and as each Mahomedan country became independent very little alteration was made. At first in Abdul Malik's time the Mahomedans feared that the "sacred name of God would be exposed to the touch of unclean persons of both sexes;" but this was overcome, and the fact remains that for hundreds of years Mahomedan coins contained the Mahomedan creed that "There is but one God and that Mahomed is His prophet." These coins found their way to India in the way of trade, and also by means of conquest; but the only part of India ever ruled direct from Damascus or Bagdad was Sind and Mooltan. Now-a-days the coins of the khalifas are found in Bombay, Sind, the Punjab, and Kandahar. Dr. DuCunha of Bombay had in his superb collection over eleven hundred of these coins in gold and silver, besides more than seven hundred and fifty Sassanian coins. These coins are interesting to our Mahomedan fellow-subjects in India, and should have been secured for the museums of the country. Unfortunately no one in authority in India knew of the sale of these coins in London, and so they were dispersed, realising for the indefatigable and learned collector scarcely their intrinsic value. Mr. Eugene Leggett of Karachi had, and may have still, a remarkably good collection of coins of the khalifas, in which, in the silver series, scarcely a year is missing from eighty-one to 308 H. No one who has not tried to collect a series of coins, in which each year and each mint shall be represented, knows the trouble and labour coin-hunting entails on one who devotes himself to this sport. You have perhaps fifty consecutive years except one. Heaps of coins are brought to you, and you go through them with the hope the missing year may turn up. But it does not, though perhaps new and interesting coins may be found. In many cases Mr. Leggett, who is blind, obtained coins from several mints, struck in the same year. Enthusiasm bridges over almost insuperable difficulties. When rival khalifas set themselves up in Egypt, although the style of the coinage was changed, the spirit of the coins of Damascus and Bagdad was kept up. The confession of faith remained. But it was not to be expected that constant contact with Europe and its image-bearing coins would be without result on the coinage of the Musalmans. We accordingly find that Salah-ud-din (Salladin of crusade renown) had on some of his coins his own image on one side and the figure of a lion on the other, but this was 550 years after the death of Mahomed. The Cairo coins of this hero are strictly orthodox.

About the same time there seemed to be great laxity all over Syria and Western Asia about images on coins. Old Grecian, Roman, and Byzantium coins were copied, and Christ and the Virgin, as well as emperors, figured on the coins of the Mahomedans. A hundred years later, a dynasty called Bani Rasul, which ruled in Yemen, round about Aden and in Southern Arabia, had images of fishes, birds, and dogs on their coins. These were, however, the exceptions to the rule. Mahomedan coins generally are covered with Arabic inscriptions only. It may be thought that they afford but little interest to the collector. On the contrary, the fact that they give us the year in which they were struck in nearly every case, that they often give us the name of the mint town, and that on the later coins we find not only the name of the ruler, the khalifa who struck them, but also that of the man in charge of the mint, is sufficient, in the absence of mint records, to make the collector most eager to possess every specimen he can lay his hands on.

When the khalifas became mere expensive ornaments, who took no part in the administration of the empire (which had in fact been wrested from them), the real rulers still struck coins bearing their names. These real rulers, although all power was in their hands, eagerly sought for titles from these puppet pontiffs; and although the coins of the khalifas struck by themselves are not found, still their names appear on the coins of those to whom they had given titles. We shall have occasion to notice instances of this in our papers on the coins of the Mahomedan rulers of India, and also when we come to consider the coins of the Hon'ble East India Company.

The fact that the khalifas lived from 632 *A. D.* to 1258 *A. D.*, and that they were the temporal as well as religious rulers of the Mahomedan world, must always make the study of their coins one not only of interest, but of necessity to the historian and archæologist. Again, the fact that they were imitated by many independent rulers in the far-off outskirts of the Mahomedan empire increases the interest in them. Every alteration in the inscriptions is some addition to our stock of knowledge, while every date and every mint town given adds only to the accuracy of the materials we may obtain from them.

It is rather humiliating to us to be obliged to confess that in no Indian museum is there anything like a collection of coins of the khalifas, although India is the only civilised government in Asia, and although the Mahomedan subjects of the British empire in India number more than those under any one government in the whole world. We know of no Mahomedan gentleman, or ruler, or student in India who has any of these coins. Yet nothing could be more interesting to the Musalman, for these coins show the handwriting current in the first century of the Hijira, and must, therefore, give the very style in which the first Quran was written. To the Christian these coins are extremely interesting, as they show us plainly what form of doctrine the Musalmans were attacking, and how *they* understood that doctrine.

VIII.

IN our last paper we said the khalifas of Bagdad ceased to exist in 1258 *A. D.*, and that the only part of India they ever conquered and ruled was Sind and Multan. Sind was subdued in 712 *A. D.*, in the time of the khalifa Walid. "The conquest of Sind took place at the very time in which, at the opposite extremes of the known world, the Mahomedan arms were subjugating Spain, and pressing on the southern frontier of France, while they were adding Khwarazin to their already mighty empire. In Sind, as in Spain, where submission was proffered, quarter was readily given; the people of the country were permitted the exercise of their own creed and laws; and natives were sometimes placed in responsible situations of the Government." Of course all this implies that the countries between Sind and Bagdad had already been conquered. Conflicting accounts are given as to the extent of the conquest; some authorities going so far as to say that the whole of Northern India was subdued as far as Kanauj eastwards and the foot of the Kashmir hills northwards. The conqueror, Mahomed Kasim, was recalled in 715 *A. D.* after a stay in India of 3¼ years. Governors were sent to Sind. Yazid, who succeeded Mahomed Kasim, died 18 days after his arrival in the country. After him Habib was appointed.

Communication was not rapid in those days, and the Sindians took advantage of the delays, caused by the roads, on the arrival of the new governor, to revolt ; but they were subdued to some extent, for we read of the "command of the Sind frontier." Nevertheless the provinces conquered originally never came back into their hands, and "the settlements were not so far in advance as they had been previously." On the occasion of the first conquest many of the Sindians had become Mahomedans, but they subsequently relapsed into idolatry. In Elliot's *History of India*, Volume I., we have extracts from the work of Al Biladuri's account of the "Conquests of Sind," and in them the names of Amru, Abdur Rahman, Hasham, Umr, Daud, as governors of the country. In the Appendix to the same volume we have other names—Ali, Amrau, Mahamed and others. Sind was ruled by the Mahomedan khalifas until the year 870 *A. D.* It then became an outlying province of the ruler of Balkh and Turkistan, and finally became independent about 879 *A. D.*

We have but few coins of these governors of Sind, but they are always turning up in driblets. They are mostly of silver, and are smaller in size than the English silver penny. Twenty or twenty-one go to a rupee in weight. They are covered with Arabic inscriptions, three lines on each side, and of course on such small coins there are no margins. They give us the names of the governors, and in some cases of the clans of the governors, the governor's name being preceded by the word *banu*, sons. On some the title "Amir" comes along with the name—as Amir Abdur Rahman, Amir Abdullah, The whole of these coins are, however, of the deepest interest to the historian, as they are the first Mahomedan coins struck *in India*, and tney give us the names of men long, long since forgotten. Indeed some names on the coins are not mentioned by the historian. There are some coins in copper. They give the name of the mint sometimes—Mansura, a place built by the Sind governors as a place of safety. The silver coins nearly always have the creed of Islam on them. There seem to be no coins of the time of independence, either before or after the times of the governors, from which we may infer that the Sindians relapsed into the condition of low civilisation in which they had previously rejoiced. Notices of these coins of the governors of Sind are to be found in the *Indian Antiquary* and in *The Dynasty of the Guptas in India* by Edward Thomas. The Lahore Museum will shortly possess the best known collection of Sind coins.

The coins of the khalifas of which we wrote in our last paper tell us that Merv, Bukhara, Samarkand, and Balkh were early brought under the sway of Islam. These towns are all in what is known as Turkistan. Their glory has long since passed away, and their present condition can be ascertained from the pages of Vambéry, Curzon, and Le Messurier. In no case did the khalifas rule over these cities two hundred years. The truth is that the conquests of the early leaders of Mahomedanism secured so much plunder and solid wealth that those who succeeded to it needed only time to work their own ruin. It is not good for man to have an indefinite amount of wealth at his disposal and have nothing to do but spend it. Luxury in the end brings ruin. It is no wonder then that the ruler of Turkistan became independent. The first ruler whom historians recognise as the Amir of Turkistan received from the khalifa a diploma investing him with sovereign powers in a somewhat remarkable fashion. His name was Ismael and his family name Saman, hence he is known as Ismael Samani. The khalifa had determined to destroy him, and to that end had sent a celebrated general against him. This general was defeated, and Ismael sent him to the khalifa, who imprisoned him and put him to death, and then sent to Ismael the diploma appointing him ruler in Turkistan. There is nothing succeeds like success. This was about the year 900 *A. D.* Fifty years before this the mints of the towns mentioned above had ceased to strike coins in the name of the khalifas. This shows, therefore, that for a period of half a century struggles had been going on in Turkistan between the khalifas and the real rulers. The latter were at last successful and were recognised as sovereigns, and then *they* began to strike coins. These coins in gold, silver, and copper followed the orthodox style of Mahomedan, always having the *kalima* on them, but adding the names of the sovereigns who struck them. There were in all ten of these Samani sovereigns, reckoning Ismael's father. They reigned about a hundred years. They did not rule in Turkistan only, but extended their conquests over Afghanistan, Eastern Persia, and Chinese Tartary. The usual thing happened; the governors of distant provinces became independent. As early as 976 *A. D.* Subaktagin became the recognised sovereign of Ghazni. He had been only a Turki slave, but slaves in those days had chances of having their merits recognised, and as Subaktagin was a man of genius and energy, he came naturally to the front, and his low origin forms a good background of the picture wherein are depicted his doughty deeds. On his coins he always acknowleged fealty to the last Samani ruler, Mansur-bin-Nuh. The son of Subaktagin was Mahmud, who succeeded his father in 998 *A. D.*, after setting aside his brother Ismael. Before saying anything further of Mahmud we may as well state that the coins of the Samanis and of Turkistan during the century of their rule are found in fair quantities. They record in metal the many changes which occurred in Turkistan in that period. Not only did outlying provinces revolt: changes took place in the country itself. The coins give us the names of the mint towns, the date and the names of the successful rebels, so that with their aid alone we can state who was ruling at Samarkand, or Bukhara, or Balkh in a certain year, and thus make out an outline of events as they happened. To go into details would be beyond the province of this paper. The second volume of the British Museum catalogue of Oriental coins gives further particulars, but a fuller and more interesting sketch was written in the journal of the Asiatic Society of Bengal by Mr. E. E. Oliver of Lahore in 1886. The three plates of coins which illustrate his paper were made from coins obtained in India.

Mahmud of Ghazni is well known to every school-boy in the Punjab, as is his father Subaktagin. The latter was the first Musalman invader of the Punjab from the North-West. Mahmud, however, conquered the whole of Northern India, from Kanauj to Gujerat. The story of his conquests may be read in every history of India. He died in 1030 *A. D.*, thirty-six years before William the Conqueror defeated Harold in the battle of Hastings. He reigned thirty-two years, and during all that time was scarcely ever at peace. He came some sixteen times to India, and each time destroyed many cities and returned home laden with their wealth and with slaves. The latter were so cheap in Ghazni that one could be bought for a rupee. Up to the present day the old towns of the Punjab bear marks of these incursions. The wealth Mahmud acquired from his predatory incursions enabled him to strike a large amount of coin in gold, silver, and copper. His coinage indicates the growth of his empire. One series of coins he struck in Lahore. On one side in the centre was the Mahomedan confession of faith, together with the name and titles of Mahmud; on the margin was a statement of the fact that the coin was struck at Mahmudpur as it pleased the conqueror to re-name Lahore, and the year. The other side was covered with Sanskrit. In the centre it was stated that the Invisible was One, his incarnation Mahomed, and *the* king Mahmud. The margin had the same meaning as the other one, but was in Sanskrit. So far as we know, this was the first use of Sanskrit on a Mahomedan coin. Its use was evident, and need not be commented on. Mahmud had a younger brother with whom he lived in peace. He was ruler of Seistan, or Sejistan as the coins have it. Coins were struck in that country with the name of the brother Nasr on one side and that of Mahmud on the other. These coins are very rare, but the coins of Mahmud are exceedingly numerous, and are found in great variety in silver; the gold and copper coins are much rarer.

Mahmud had two sons, Masaud and Muhammad, twins, of whom the former was born first. Masaud was warlike, almost too much of a soldier to please his father, and he being absent when his father died, Muhammad took the throne; but he held it for a short time, for Masaud wrenched it from him, put him in prison, and blinded him. Masaud reigned for ten years, from 1030 to 1040 *A. D.* He often invaded India, and during one of these incursions took the fort of Hansi, which up to that time had resisted successfully all attempts to take it. The coins of Masaud are common in silver. Maudud succeeded his father Masaud. During his reign coins were struck at Lahore, which had on one side the couchant bull which the Brahmin kings of Kabul, Samanta Deva, Syalapati, Bhim Deva, and another king had struck on their coins. The coins of Maudud had on them the name of Samanta Deva over the bull. The other side had in the centre the name and titles of Maudud, and in the margin a legend to the effect that the coin was struck in Lahore (or Lohor as it was spelt on the coins) and the year. There are many of these coins, as there are also of those struck in the Ghazni fashion. These Lahore coins are always of base metal. The use of the bull and the Hindu name is the first conversion of the Mahomedans to Hinduism, and these coins are probably the first Mahomedan coins with images on them. The rest of the Ghazni kings followed the example set by Maudud. The only interest the coins possess is their inscriptions. The story of all these sovereigns is thoroughly Oriental. The upshot of things was that Ghazni was burnt down and plundered. Lahore was used as a place of refuge by the last king but one of this dynasty—Khusrau Shah. His son, Khusrau Malik, took up his residence permanently at Lahore, and there struck coins. Khusrau Shah reigned from 1152 to 1160 *A. D.* His son from 1160 to 1187, when he surrendered to Mahomed Gauri. The coins of Ibrahim of Ghazni, who reigned from 1059 to 1099, are very numerous in silver and billon, but only one gold coin is known ; it is in the Lahore

Museum. One series of coins is worthy of mention. They have both the bull and horseman of the coins of the Kabuli kings on them, but over the horseman comes sometimes the name of Maudud or Masaud or Mahmud or Muhammad. They are very rare indeed, and must be from some Indian mint.

The Ghazni dynasty lasted over 200 years. Great results followed the conquest of India by Mahmud and his successors. It is this which gives so much interest to the coins of the Ghaznivides. Their many types and their varied inscriptions make them interesting to the numismatist and the historian. No one who wants to know about the first Mahomedan conquerors of India can afford to neglect them. A good collection of them is essential to every Indian museum.

IX.

TWO hundred years is a long time. Since 1691 many events have happened in India in connection with the growth of a foreign power in the country. The two hundred years during which the Ghaznivides influenced Northern India were also fruitful in events. The result of all was this, that in India one Mahomedan power was overthrown by another Mahomedan power, and the victor had then to conquer the rulers of Native States who had not been previously conquered by the first conquerors. Muiz-ud-din Muhammad-bin-Sam, brother of Gyas-ud-din Muhammad-bin-Sam, was the general who conquered Khusrau Malik, the last Ghaznivide sovereign, who was, however, the first of that dynasty to take up his permanent residence in India. He is commonly known as Muhammad Gauri. After he had taken Khusrau Malik prisoner at Lahore he was obliged to meet the combined forces of Hindustan proper. In the first battle he was defeated and was forced to return to Ghazni, but coming back the next year he crushed the combined forces of Delhi and Ajmir at Narain or Tarauri, a place north of Sirsa and Bhatinda, for it was to these places the conqueror pursued the defeated forces. Prithvi, raja of Ajmir, was slain. Muhammad Gauri afterwards extended his conquests over the whole of Northern India, but

Plate IV

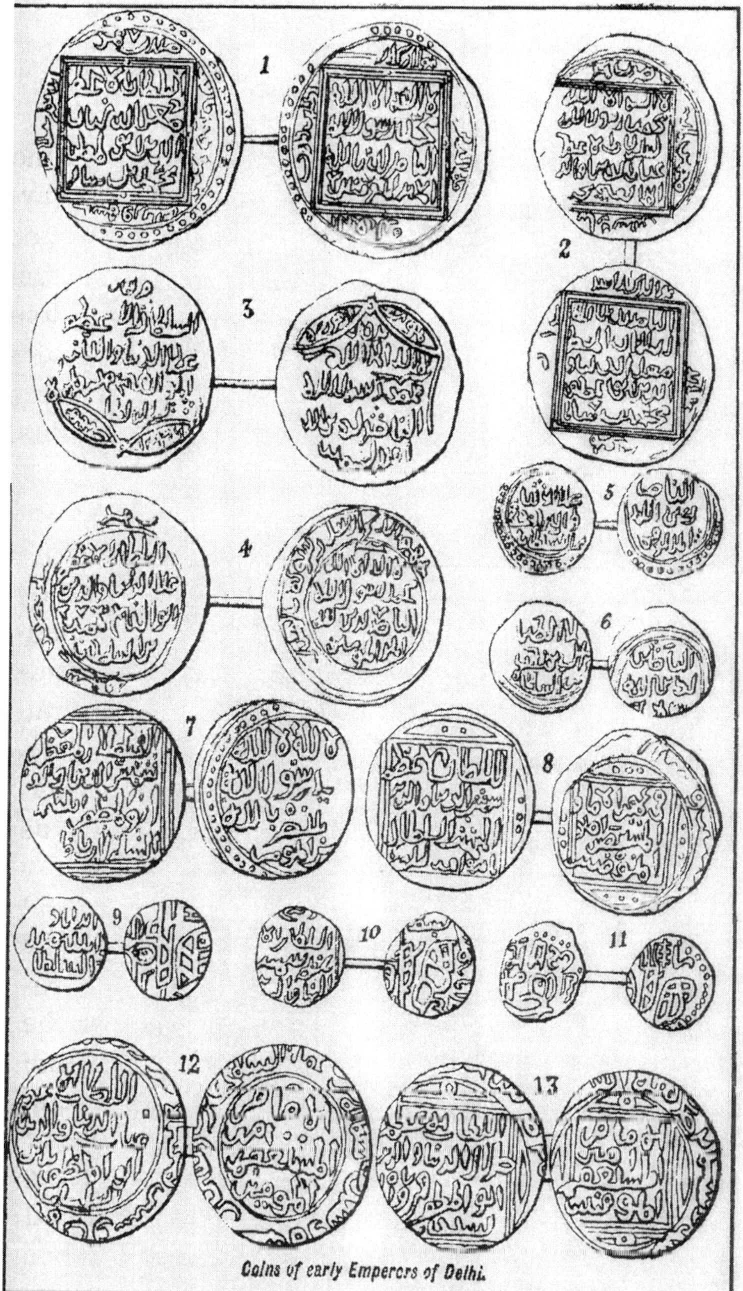

Coins of early Emperors of Delhi.

was killed in his own tent at last by the Ghakkars, on the banks of the Indus. He had reigned in India from 1193 to 1205 *A. D.* His coins in gold, silver, and copper, or rather a mixture of copper and silver, are well known. The gold is rare, so is the silver, but the coins in mixed metals are numerous. On the gold and silver coins we have the name of the elder brother Gyas-ud-din, along with Muiz-ud-din's name. On some of these coins the inscriptions are in concentric circles, on others in square areas with margins. The billon coins are in the greatest variety. Some of them have the bull on one side and the horseman on the other. Over the bull is the name "Muhammad Sam" in Hindi letters. Over the horse is "Sri Hamira" also in Hindi. This coin shows that the conqueror was bent on having his name known as ruler. At the same time the use of the bull and horseman shows that he was ready to make concessions to his new subjects. The coin is similar to the one that Prithvi Raja had struck. Another coin rarely found has on the one side "Muhammad Sam" in Hindi and on the other over the horseman "Prithvi Raja." This was probably struck to show that Muhammad Sam had taken the place of Prithvi Raja. Another coin has on one side the Arabic word "Adl," justice, and on the other "Muiz." The use of this word "*Adl*" is curious. The East India Company put it on their copper coins in connection with a pair of scales, and as justice is always represented as holding a pair of scales, the meaning of the Company was probably that their rule was one of justice. But on the coin of Muhammad Sam it probably means *an equivalent*, or a legal and authorised tender or currency. The word was often used by succeeding kings, and always in connection with their titles or names, thus, "Adl-i-Sultan," "Zarb-i-Multan;" "Adl-i-Feroz Shaḥ," "Zarb-i-Delhi," &c. One series of coins struck in gold at Kanauj has on one side the image of the goddess Lakhshmi and on the other the name of "Muhammad Sam" stamped after the fashion of the preceding rulers of Kanauj.

One of Muhammad Sam's generals was Yalduz. He struck coins on which was the name of his master and his own, coupled nearly always with the statement that he was his master's slave. Yalduz followed the fashion of his master and struck coins, using both the bull and horseman. Some historians talk about the bull and horseman dynasty. This is of course quite wrong. We have seen that the bull and horseman were first used by the Brahmin kings of Kabul, then by the later Ghaznivides, and now we see that Muhammad Sam and Yalduz use them. Succeeding kings also kept them on their coins. Native rajas nearly always used them. It was a wise concession on the part of the conquerors not to alter altogether the coinage to which India had become accustomed.

Qutb-ud-din Aibak succeeded Muhammad Sam. He reigned five years, but none of his coins are known. His son Aram Shah reigned part of a year, and only one small kind of copper is known of his. The Qutb at Delhi was commenced by Muhammad-bin-Sam, and probably finished by Qutb-ud-din Aibak. That pillar of victory with its Arabic inscriptions showed the people of India who their rulers were.

Aibak had been a slave of Muhammad-bin-Sam. Aibak's slave, Shams-ud-din Altamsh, put aside Aram Shah and seated himself on the throne of his master's son, on which he sat for a quarter of a century—a fact which shows that he must have been a man of genius and power, one born to rule. He had a hard time of it. Nasir-ud-din Qubacha disputed his rights in the Punjab: Nasir-ud-din Qurlagh in parts of the same province. Bengal, which had been conquered in the time of Muhammad-bin-Sam, revolted, and had to be subdued. The whole of Northern India was at times in a state of ferment. Finally, however, Altamsh died and was neither murdered nor slain in battle. Of his coins many have been preserved down to our time. One coin only is known in gold, but his silver pieces of nearly 170 grains are occasionally met with. These latter contain on one side the Kalima and the name of the khalifa of Bagdad, Al Mustansir, who sent an emissary to Delhi on a visit to Altamsh. (He probably brought a sanad, conferring on Altamsh the sovereignty of India, much the same as the Pope gave to Portugal nearly four hundred years ago. For this, of course, an adequate return in hard cash would have to be made to the khalifa); the other side of the coin contained the name and titles of Altamsh. The billon and copper coins of Altamsh are numerous and in great variety. Sometimes both bull and horseman are used and only Hindi inscriptions. Sometimes the horseman occupies one side and an Arabic inscription the other. Sometimes both sides are covered with Arabic.

On the north-western borders there were troubles. Ala-ud-din, the great king of Khwarizm, and his son, Jalal-ud-din, were there. Later on Changez Khan, the great conqueror, threatened India. The coins of all these are frequently found; Ala-ud-din's in great abundance. Jalal-ud-din's are often in Hindi only, with the horseman and bull. The coins of Qubacha and of Nasir-ud-din Qurlagh are also often met with. So that the reign of Altamsh may easily be represented by means of coins. Collectors will be glad to know that new types of the coins of this king are often turning up. No one can collect for long without bringing something new to light. "Altamsh" is the name by which this sovereign is generally known, but it is pretty certain that was not his real name. "Eltitmish" seems to be on some coins. Major Raverty writes it, however, "I-yal-timish," but the Major is not always correct, for it has been proved that the coin, whose inscriptions he gives in his notes, could never have been in existence.

Altamsh was succeeded by his son Rukn-ud-din Feroz Shah, but as he gave himself up to low pleasures and degrading vices he was soon dethroned. His coins are exceedingly rare, but still several types are known, although we have no gold or silver coin of his.

Razia, the daughter of Altamsh, then ascended the throne. Her only fault seems to have been that she was a woman. As a woman she fell in love, and the object of her favour was an Abyssinian. This did not please her nobles, all of whom were probably descendants of slaves. In the fourth year of her reign she and her lover went to Bhatinda to put down the governor of that important fort, who was in rebellion. The lover was killed and the queen imprisoned by the governor, who, however, later on, made her an inmate of his zenana. The queen with her new lover then attempted a movement towards Delhi to recover power, but near Kaithal they were both slain. The coins of this ill-fated queen are exceedingly rare. A few rupees are known, but no gold coins. Those in copper and billon are seldom met with, and in consequence command a high price. Of late years several new types have been brought to light. One new type has the word "Razia" in Arabic in a rayed circle, and on the other side the sitting bull, with an inscription over it in Hindi. Another has the same word only inverted as in type. Further research will be almost sure to bring more types to light, for in all probability she imitated the coinage of her father. Her coins are of the greatest interest, as she was the only queen who ever ruled in India before the accession of our own beloved Queen-

Empress. She died in 1239 *A. D.*, and was succeeded by her younger brother, who reigned only two years, and was succeeded by his nephew, a son of Rukn-ud-din Feroz. He reigned five years and was succeeded by a son of Altamsh, named Nasir-ud-din Mahmud Shah, who held the throne from 1246 to 1265 *A. D.* Although he reigned so long he was a man scarcely fitted for the rough times in which his lot was cast. Revolts were rife in the land. The Moguls began also to make incursions into the Punjab. The emperor employed himself in writing Qurans, which he sold, and the price of which he lived on, his empress cooking his meals. One of his nobles, Ulugh Khan, was his son-in-law, and he was made of different stuff. Fortunately for India the Quran-copying king died without male issue, and his martial son-in-law succeeded him, assuming the title and name of Gyas-ud-din Balban. He reigned from 1265 to 1287. His first act was to destroy all the slave-nobles who wielded so much power. Then he gave his attention to the formation of a disciplined army. Delhi becoming thus a place of safety, numerous men of learning flocked to it. Rebellions were put down in Mewat and Bengal. The Moguls, however, still continued their incursions, and it was in successfully resisting one of these that the king's beloved son, Prince Muhammad, was slain. Balban was then an old man of about eighty. The shock was too much for him, and in two years afterwards he died. The coins of this king and of his three predecessors do not differ much. The Kalima was not on them, but on one side were the name and titles of the king and on the other the name of the khalifa. *Both* sides of both rupees and mohurs had a margin, which contained the name of the mint and the year, in Arabic words. Gold coins of Mahmud are known, but are very rare. Balban's are met with more frequently. Rupees of both, in good condition with margins complete, are very scarce. Balban was the last who employed the horseman on his coins. Only one coin of his of this type is known. Balban introduced a new type of copper coin. In the centre, in a circle, was the word "Balban" in Arabic: round it "Gyas-ud-din Sultan" in Hindi. The other side was covered with Arabic. The copper coins of Balban are common, and are of several types.

Balban was succeeded by his grandson Kaikubad, the son of a son of Balban, who was ruling over Bengal. He was a young man who was not equal to the post to which he had been elevated. He gave himself to pleasure, so his wazir or prime minister poisoned him, and reigned in his stead, *i. e.*, he at first set up a puppet king, Kaiumours, for three months, and then seated himself on the throne. A nephew of Balban, Malik Chhaju, got up a rebellion, but it was put down. Coins of Kaikubad are common, except in gold. *One* rupee is know of Kaiumours, and it would seem that Chhaju showed his relationship to royalty by coining. The wazir called himself Jalal-ud-din Feroz Shah. He reigned from 1290 to 1295. His coins are common in silver and copper, but only two or three are known in gold. They follow the types of Balban. Feroz Shah employed his nephew in the conquest of the Dekkan; this was the first time that that part of India was brought under Mahomedan rule. The wealth obtained by the plunder of the Dekkan enabled the nephew to keep up a large army, so he thought himself strong enough to murder his uncle and seize the throne. This he did in 1295 *A. D.* For a short time, however, a young prince, Rukn-ud-din Ibrahim, son of Feroz Shah, was placed on the throne, only to be driven away and finally murdered at Bohar near Rohtak. One rupee of this prince is known, but his copper coins are of three types, each one of which is of course rare.

The nephew of Feroz Shah called himself Ala-ud-din Muhammad Shah. He was a strong, unscrupulous man, and reigned twenty years, *i. e.*, till 1315 *A. D* His coins are very common in gold, silver, and copper; but gold and silver, with the margin on one side complete, are not so frequently met with. One of his copper coins, with Muhammad Shah in a circle, had a margin in Hindi, in which the date is also in Hindi figures. This is the first and almost only case in which the date is given in Hindi. Every year's coins may be obtained by the patient collector. The other copper coins did not vary from those of his predecessors. Ala-ud-din did a lot of work at the Qutb near Delhi. His gateway is nearly perfect to the present time. The lofty arches there are also his work.

X.

WE learn from the historians of the last king whom we mentioned, Ala-ud-din Muhammad Shah, what the prices of things were. Up to his time no one thought of recording this, to us, most interesting fact. The maund was then about 28lb. A maund of wheat could be purchased for about 3 annas 10 pies, or about 11 annas for the maund of the present day. Sugar cost 2¼ farthings per seer. Salt sold at the rate of about 8 pies for 35 seers. Up to this time, however, we meet with no statement as to the relative values of gold and silver. Plunder from the Dekkan must have made gold cheaper in and about Delhi. One thing, however, we see, the gold and silver coins were of the same weight. We do not know how many of the copper coins went to a rupee, nor how many of the billon coins, which are a mixture of silver and copper, with the amount of silver varying in the coins of each year. Striking a bargain with such a medium of exchange must have been a work of many words and much time.

After the death of Ala-ud-din everything went wrong. His eldest son was set aside and murdered. A young child was placed on the throne with the title and name of Shihab-ud-din Umar, and prince Mubarak was appointed regent. The latter blinded the former in the fortress of Gwalior, and himself ascended the throne, taking the name of Qutb-ud-din Mubarak Shah. He was only seventeen. His reign of four years was one of peace, but the emperor was perhaps the most debauched person who ever disgraced a throne. He nevertheless called himself the khalifa of Almighty God, and on his coins he never put the name of the khalifa of Bagdad. Assuming this title he called Delhi Dar-ul-Khilafat, the abode of the khalifa—a title which in later times was given to other cities of India. This king was the first Musalman king of India to make square coins. They are found in gold, silver, and copper. His billon coins are numerous: but the gold and silver, round and square, are very rare. He was murdered in 1320 *A.D.* His murderer was a man of low caste, but he not only seized the throne, he possessed himself of his master's harem. He called himself Nazir-ud-din Khusrau Shah. Within a year he was defeated and murdered. His coins are of necessity very rare, but they are known in gold, silver, and billon.

During the reign of Mubarak Shah a coin was struck bearing the name of Shams-ud-din Mahmud Shah. We don't know who he was. In the second year of his reign the emperor went a tour in the Dekkan. He took a cousin with him and left Delhi in the hands of one of his creatures. When returning he suddenly ordered his cousin to be executed, and when he arrived in Delhi the same fate was measured out to the man who had been left as governor of that city. It is surmised that the cousin and the governor were plotting for the throne. The coin was evidently struck in Delhi. The king probably saw it, and as it bore on it the year of his absence he imagined that, either the governor or his cousin, or both, were plotting against him. No mention is made of Shams-ud-din Mahmud Shah in history. His name and date are found only on one known coin. If more coins could be obtained we might get to know more about him.

The conqueror of Khusrau Shah had been governor of Multan. He ascended the throne as Gyas-ud-din Shah Tuglaq Shah in 1320 *A. D.* He was a wise king and introduced many beneficial changes. Successful expeditions were sent to the Dekkan, and the king himself headed one to Bengal. Dekkan affairs were in the hands of the king's son. When the king returned from Bengal his son was acting viceroy at Delhi. He erected a pavilion in which to receive his father with honour, but it was so constructed that when the emperor stepped into it the whole erection fell on him and killed him. This was in 1325 *A. D.*

This king's coins are plentiful in gold, silver, billon, and copper, and are of several types in each metal. Some were struck at Deogir, others at Talang, both in the Dekkan. The son and murderer caused coins to be struck on which the father is called the *martyred* Sultan. While the emperor was in Bengal, rupees were struck on which was his own name and the name of the governor of Bengal whom he went to chastise. The emperor's name, of course, occupies the place of honour.

The murderer of his father ascended the throne as Muhammad, the son of Tuglaq, and he reigned till 1351 *A. D.* He was learned, merciless, religious, and mad. His acts show this. He ordered all the inhabitants of Delhi to go to Deogir. He ordered an army of 100,000 horse to enter the Himalayas and conquer China. He ordered copper and brass coins to be struck and to be put in circulation as gold. And yet it is as a moneyer that numismatists regard Muhammad Tuglaq, for his coins in gold, silver, billon, and copper are in greater variety, and have more varied inscriptions than those of any other king of India. The inscriptions are, moreover, in better condition, and this implies that the dies were better made. Some of the gold coins are nearly 200 grains in weight. One goes up to 245 grains. The gold and silver coins give the mints of Delhi, Sultanpur in the Dekkan, Satgaon, Sonargaon, and Laknauti in Bengal. On small silver coins, weighing a little more than 50 grains, he gives himself all kinds of titles—the Just ; the Earnest in the way of God ; the Patient Waiter on the mercy of God ; the Victorious by the help of God, &c. On his copper coins he states that " He who obeys the Sultan obeys God," and " Obey God and the Prophet and those in authority among you," for " Sovereignty is not conferred on every man, but some are placed over others." On another coin he calls himself " The Sultan, the Shadow of God."

Knowing that he was the murderer of his father he sought to be recognised as emperor of India by the khalifa of Egypt. When that recognition was given he struck coins in India from which his own name was banished, and on which was the name and titles of the khalifa. These are in gold, silver, billon, and copper. Many are dated. Three khalifas' names appear on the coins—Sulaiman, Ahmad, and Al Mastakfi.

This emperor succeeded to more of India than any of his predecessors, and it was during his reign disintegration set in. The Dekkan slipped out of his hands altogether, and Bengal became independent. The story of the man who became the founder of the Bahmani kingdom in the Dekkan is worth repeating, as it has to do with a find of gold coins. His name was Saiyid Ahsan Shah, and he was a native of Kaithal. Not finding employment near home he went to Delhi, where he got work under a man named Bahman Kanko or Gango. One day when ploughing a field the share of the plough struck on a vessel which proved to be full of gold coins. He at once took all of them to his master, who was delighted with his honesty. The fame of the deed reached the son of the then king, the first Tuglaq. He knowing how scarce honest men were, gave him a small post in the army. Ahsan gradually rose in favour and in power, until at last he was made a general and sent in command of an army to the Dekkan. There he watched events for the king and himself. Seeing the king's power growing weaker and weaker he bided his time, and at last seized Kulburga and proclaimed himself independent, striking coins in his own name and changing the name of his capital to Ahsanabad now called Hasanabad. He always called himself Ahsan Shah Bahmani after his Delhi master. Muhammad Tuglaq had his revenge: in one of his expeditions he slew all the Saiyids of Kaithal. The dynasty founded by Ahsan Shah and called after him Bahmani, lasted, however, two hundred years. Muhammad Tuglaq died in Sind of a fever contracted by eating too much fish, *A. D.* 1351.

He was succeeded by his nephew Feroz Shah Tuglaq, who, if his uncle may be called the "Prince of Moneyers," may be called the "Prince of Builders." While, however, Feroz was coming up from Sind to Delhi, a long march in those days, a boy was put on the throne in Delhi, and gold and silver coins were struck in his name—Gyas-ud-din Mahmud Shah. When Feroz arrived in Delhi the boy was deposed and put out of sight. Feroz Shah's reign was a long one, from 1351 to 1388 *A. D.*, thirty-eight years according to Mahomedan reckoning. He was a great builder of mosques, and tombs, and bridges, and he also repaired many old buildings. He built the city of Hissar, using materials he stole from Agroha in its construction. Many other places regard him as their founder, such as Ferozpore in the Punjab; and Sirhind was made by him the head-quarters of a division. It was nothing before his time. It is important to note this latter fact, because historians often mention a Sirhind near Sirsa. This should be *Bhatinda*, not Sirhind. Careful writers, such as Sir Alexander Cunningham and Edward Thomas, have made the mistake however.

Feroz Shah's coins are numerous and varied in gold, billon, and copper; but his silver coins are exceedingly rare. In copper and billon he imitated some of the coins of his uncle. Both his sons, Fath and Zafar, died before him, but their names are associated with their father's on a series of coins. There is a posthumous series of copper coins of Feroz Shah's. The dates show that coins bore the name of Feroz Shah for nearly forty years after his death. Coins in billon of every year of Feroz Shah's reign are obtainable.

After Feroz Shah's death in 1388 *A. D.* there was considerable confusion in the country. Tuglaq Shah II. reigned a short time and was killed. The son of prince Zafar, by name Abu Bakr, shared the same fate in 1389 *A. D.* Muhammad, son of Feroz Shah, then ascended the throne and managed to keep it till 1392, when his son, Sikandar, succeeded him and reigned forty-five days. He was succeeded by Mahmud Shah, who from 1392 to 1412 *A. D.* was king in name; another man, Nasrat Shah, being also king at the same time. Coins of all these kings are known. Of Sikandar, who reigned forty-five days only, at least coins of six types are to be found in billon. Gold and billon coins of all the rest are known. When they put a khalifa's name on their coins it was that of Abu Abdulla, who died five years before Feroz Shah, showing that the name of a khalifa only was wanted to give colouring to the authority of the king.

During this confusion Jaunpur became an independent kingdom, and coins began to be struck there before Mahmud Shah died. It was during the time of the quarrel between Nasrat Shah and Mahmud Shah that the terrible invasion of India by Taimur (Timurlane or Timurlang) took place. Delhi was sacked and the inhabitants were massacred. After his departure the confusion in Delhi was perfect. Mahmud was reinstated and for some years was king in name over a nominal kingdom. One poor small copper coin of Taimur struck at Delhi is known.

On the death of Mahmud, Daulat Khan, Khizr Khan, Mubarak Shah, Muhammad Shah, and Alam Shah reigned until 1451 *A. D.* Of the first two no coins are known, but the last three are well represented. The coins of the last two are important, as Muhammad's coins show the name of his father and grandfather, and Alam's coins that of his father.

It was time a vigorous man came forward to manage affairs, for of course distant provinces like Gujerat and Malwa had become independent. Bahlol Lodhi, a governor of the Punjab, came to the front. Alam Shah vacated the throne and retired to Budaon, where he employed himself in gardening. Bahlol hated pomp, and was satisfied to know and feel himself king. He was a strong man and re-annexed Jaunpur to his dominions. His rule, therefore, extended only over the Punjab, Hindustan proper, and Jaunpur. Bengal, the Dekkan, Gujerat, and Malwa were lost to the empire.

Bahlol's coins of seven or eight types are known : none are in gold or silver. Three series are dated, and a patient collector by visiting all the bazaars of Northern India might get a coin of every year of his reign. Some of his billon coins contain only a trace of silver, others as much as five or six grains, and some contain as much as fifteen grains, a beautiful currency for making a bargain with!

Sikandar Lodhi succeeded his father in 1488 and reigned till 1517 *A. D.* His coinage is only in billon and copper, and of only three or four types. His large billon coins have been assayed, and it has been shown that they contain from 1½ to 32 grains of silver each.

Ibrahim Lodhi succeeded Sikandar, his father, and reigned till 1526 *A. D.* His coins are by far the worst in execution from the time of Muhammad-bin-Sam. They seem to show that some change was needful in the management of the empire. They are almost all small, scarcely even dated, and never have more than a small portion of an inscription on them. A good coin of Ibrahim Lodhi's is one of the rarest things a collector can secure.

For years changes had been taking place in Turkistan. A man named Zahir-ud-din Babar had been prominent in them all. At last he rose superior to every difficulty and took Kabul. Thence he turned his attention and his arms towards India. The confusion of the empire offered an opportunity for its conquest, and stirred up some nobles to make him the offer of their assistance. Babar came, and at last on the field of Panipat defeated and slew Ibrahim, and thus became, by right of conquest, the first

Mogul emperor of India and the founder of an empire which collapsed, as all its predecessors had done, but not until it had shown that a united India might become one of the most glorious empires of the whole world when properly governed, or a scene of the wildest and most horrible confusion when its rulers gave themselves to indolence and pleasure.

XI.

OUR two last papers were on the coins of the kings of Delhi from the time that city came into the hands of Mahomedan rulers until the time of Babar, the first so-called Mogul emperor, *i. e.*, from 1193 *A. D.* to 1525 *A. D.* During this long period of over three centuries and a quarter many and great changes occurred in Central Asia and also in India. The events in Central Asia affected India, for they were the rise and fall of great families, the founders of which were conquerors. In Khwarizm, as Khiva used to be called, Ala-ud-din ruled from 1199 to 1220 *A.D.* He issued vast quantities of coins, if we may judge from the numbers which we meet with in the bazaars of Northern India. They are in gold, silver, billon, and copper. The gold and silver are mostly broad pieces. The billon and copper coins are, as a rule, small, not much larger than a two-anna piece, but copper coins are known to be the size of an eight-anna piece, and some are as broad as a rupee. The small coins have often a horse and bull on them, and some have an elephant or tapir on one side. The inscriptions are greatly diversified; in one the king calls himself the second Alexander. His mint towns were many: Herat, Ghazni, Farwan, Talikan, Kishm, Kunduz, Peshawur, Kirman, Zamindawar, Balkh, Kurzawan, Jurzuwan, Yamooz and Bamian have been noted on his coins. It is a nice exercise in geography to find these places on a map. Many new types have been found lately, and it is possible that further research will reveal many more.

Changez Khan, or Jingiz Khan, overthrew the kingdom of Ala-ud-din. He threatened India only. His conquests altered everything in Central Asia. One historian says he "built up in twenty years the widest empire the world has ever seen." He seems to have been so occupied in conquest that he gave little attention to coining, for his coins are exceedingly rare, and only a few are known in silver and copper. He was the founder of many families, however. He was himself a Mongol, or Mogul as we call it, and his empire was called the Mongol empire. He died in 1227 *A D.* "The territory he and his sons had conquered stretched from the Yellow Sea to the Crimea, from the Baikal Lake to Merv, and included lands or tribes wrung from the rule of Chinese, Tanguts, Afghans, Persians and Turks." This immense empire, of course, became divided, and Juji, Chagatai, Ogatai, and Tului, sons of Changez Khan, became founders of separate dynasties who ruled over the separate parts. The coins of these dynasties are very numerous, but not many seem to have come to India.

Taimur or Timurlang or Timurlane was descended from Chagatai. His conquests upset many dynasties. He invaded India in 1397-8 *A.D.* His massacres of prisoners, his sack of Delhi, and his cruelties are well known. He had one redeeming point: he was fond of architecture, and the buildings of old Delhi so pleased him that he took Indian artisans back with him to Samarkand that they might beautify that city. One miserable copper coin struck at Delhi is all that is now in existence to put us in mind that this merciless conqueror was once in Delhi. His coins struck in other places are, however, numerous. They are mostly large and small silver coins. The names of the mint towns on them show the extent of his conquests. The coins of the descendants of Taimur struck in Turkistan are very numerous. When he died he left 36 sons, grandsons, and great-grandsons to perpetuate his race and to quarrel amongst themselves. The son, Shah Rukh, was perhaps the greatest coiner, and his coins are constantly coming into the bazaars. He reigned 43 years and died in 1447 *A.D.*, when the great Ulugh Beg, so famous for his astronomical tables, succeeded him. The house of Taimur came to an end in 1500 *A.D.*, and Muhammad Shebani became ruler. *His* house lasted 99 years. The twelve kings composing the Shebani line have all left their coins. The house of Taimur is not only famous by reason of the deeds of its founder; one branch of it gave to the world the great Babar who became the founder of the Indian Mogul empire, of which more anon. The silver coinage of the house of Taimur and of that of Shebani is mostly composed of thin broad pieces weighing generally from about 85 to 75 grains each. One side is devoted to the Kalima and the names of the four companions of Muhammad, the other contains the name and titles of the sovereign, with name of mint town and date. One peculiar feature may be noted. The coins of former kings were often used by the ruling king, who made a stamp of much smaller size than the coin. He simply punched the coin with this, and thus deleted part of the original inscription. Coins have been found with at least three kings' names on them. These are of course very interesting. Some kings seem to have been on the throne so short a time that their own coins are not known, but they had time to re-strike the coins of others.

It was necessary to go through this brief sketch of the coins of Turkistan, because the silver coins of Babar and Humayun struck in India follow them in make and inscriptions.

We now return to India and notice what coins had been struck in other parts of the empire besides Delhi. Kashmir, surrounded as it is by mountains through which only most difficult passes penetrate, was never conquered by the Pathan emperors of Delhi. It was annexed to the empire finally by Akbar, and of that more anon. About the time of the battle of Bannockburn, *i. e.*, early in the 14th century, a Mahomedan faqir went to Kashmir, which was then ruled by a weak maharaja. He worked his way into the maharaja's favour and became tutor to his son. When the maharaja died he became prime minister and regent, for the son was not of age, and he died or was murdered before he sat on the throne. The faqir then became sole ruler of Kashmir. He married the maharaja's widow, but put her away after one night, and then as sultan Shams-ud-din struck coins in gold, silver, and copper. The silver only has come down to us. They are square and are worth intrinsically about ten annas. On one side are the name and title of the king, on the other the words Zarb-i-Kashmir (*i. e.*, struck in Kashmir) in a quatrefoil, and in the corners comes the date in Arabic *words*. There were in all about twenty sultans who reigned after Shams-ud-din. The gold coins of about four or five are known, and the copper coins of about a dozen of them. Of some Kashmiri sultans, however, no coins are known. The copper ones have a bar with a knot in the middle going across the coin. The dates are sometimes on one side in figures, but when it comes on the reverse side, it is scarcely ever legible. The later kings put the date in Persian words and figures. Zain-ul-Abidin was the greatest of these Kashmiri sultans. His silver coins always bear the date 842 A. H. (1438-9 *A. D.*). Several of his successors' coins have the same date, in either Arabic words or in figures. The chronology of these sultans is a muddle, as every historian of Kashmir makes them rulers at different times. The coins are in some cases not trustworthy, and so can give no assistance. Two kings' names come on the coins which do not come in any known history of Kashmir—Nadir Shah and Mahmud

Shah. Two kings' names come also on the coins who never reigned in Kashmir—Humayun, son of Babar, and Islam Shah Suri. Humayun's general, Mirza Haidar Doglat, conquered Kashmir while his master was an exile in Persia. The first letter of his name ح = H occurs on one coin, but as a rule Haidar used only his master's name on the Kashmir coins he struck, and thus showed that there are Orientals who prefer their master's honour to their own. The other king, Islam Shah Suri, was once invited by a faction in Kashmir to invade the country. That faction must have struck coins in Islam's name in the hope that their circulation would make their adversaries believe that he was in power, but Islam never entered the country. These silver coins of the sultans are so rare that one collector who was determined to get a specimen of each sultan, found that when he settled his accounts, each coin had cost him over twelve rupees. Several coins are known which contain names not hitherto made out. Kashmir was annexed to the Mogul empire by Akbar in the year of the Spanish Armada, 1588 *A.D.*, so that Kashmir was ruled by sultans who were Mahomedans for more than two centuries and a half. It was during this period that many of the antiquities of Kashmir were destroyed, for the father of Zain-ul-Abidin, Sikandar, earned for himself the title of But Shikan, or idol destroyer, or iconoclast. The intolerance of the Mahomedans was learned by the Hïndus, and not forgotten when the latter obtained the supremacy in the beautiful but unhappy valley. Akbar himself was tolerant and struck coins in Kashmir, exactly similar in size and make to those which had been issued by the sultans, but he also struck in Srinagar, the capital of Kashmir, rupees and dams, after the fashion of those struck in his mints all over India. Only one gold coin of Akbar struck in Kashmir is known as yet. It is square and agrees only in weight with the gold coins of the sultans. It is in the Lahore Museum.

Bengal is a long way from Delhi, but it was conquered soon after Muhammad-bin-Sam, the first Mahomedan emperor, took Delhi. From the first, however, the emperor who reigned in Delhi could have been little more than suzerain in name. Some twenty-five kings ruled over Bengal between 1202 and 1339 *A D.*, of whom some acknowledged the emperor of Delhi and some did not. The Delhi emperors had their hands full of their own affairs, and only a few could find time to go with or send armies to Bengal. Very few Bengal coins of this period are known. Perhaps, were all known cabinets searched the number would not reach twenty, and they are all silver and follow the fashion of the old Delhi silver coins. They give us, however, dates and mints, and are valuable as far as they go. From 1339 *A. D.* the sovereigns of Bengal became independent of Delhi, and had enough to do with their own concerns. Their history is thoroughly oriental. Rebellion, conquest, division, prosperity, reverses, ruin, change—

these were the lot of each family that in turn obtained the ascendancy. Thirty-one kings, of seven dynasties, ruled in the whole or a part of Bengal between 1339 and 1576 *A. D.*, when Akbar put an end to Bengali troubles by annexing the country to his empire. Of these thirty-one kings the coins of twenty-two are known in either gold or silver. They are broad pieces, somewhat lighter than the modern rupee. Their inscriptions are in Arabic, but the style of the Delhi silver coins was not followed. Dates and mints are recorded so that the coins are valuable in settling the chronology of the period. Gold coins of only a few Bengal kings are known. Within the last month, however, one was found in a Punjab bazaar, and is the first known gold coin of Shams-ud-din Muzaffar Shah. No copper coins of any Bengal kings seem to be known. This would seem to show that either the copper coinage of previous dynasties was in use, or else that small transactions were carried on by means of cowries. The coinage of these Bengal Mahomedan rulers has not yet been gone into thoroughly. No collection seems to have been made of them, and no collector seems to have made their collection a special object. They must be always coming into the bazaars of the country, and all that is wanted is that some one should draw them into his cabinet by offering a higher price for them than the silversmith. Some of the rarest of these Bengal coins have been found in the Punjab, and their presence in one part of India, remote from the mints in which they were struck, argues that they may be found near those mints as well as far away from them. There is an opening here for a Bengali gentleman of antiquarian tastes. If we remember that before the conquest of Bengal by the Mahomedans the country was ruled by Khhatri and Kaith and Vaidya rajas, the search for the coins of these dynasties might be made. Bengal must have been a rich country for centuries before its Mahomedan conquest, for mosques in Bengal erected by Musalman kings contain a great amount of materials from palaces and temples created in olden times, and it would be a wonder if those who erected those palaces and temples had no currency beyond cowries. We do not know any Bengali coin collector. Should any Bengali gentleman, however, wish to collect, we would suggest one thing only to him—he must go and hunt for the coins in the bazaars of the country. Of the coins of Nepal, Assam, Kachar, and Tibet, we must write in another paper.

XII.

THE disintegration of the Delhi empire began in the reign of Muhammad Tuglaq. That mad sovereign exhausted all his resources on impossibilities. He lost an army of over a hundred thousand horse in the gorges and mountain paths of the Himalayas in a vain attempt to conquer China. Provinces which lay remote from Delhi had to be entrusted to men who turned out more selfish than loyal. In 1294 Deogir and Elichpur were conquered by Ala-ud-din. In 1322 Tuglaq Shah I., the father of Muhammad Tuglaq, invaded Telingana. It was in 1347 *A. D.* that Ahsan Shah Gangu Bahmani saw his way to setting up his own standard at Kulburga, a place about 120 miles west of Hyderabad in the Dekkan. From this place he ruled the whole of the upper basins of the Godaveri and Kistna rivers, *i. e.*, the "greater part of the present Bombay Presidency south of Surat, and most of the Nizam's dominions." This kingdom is known in history as the *Bahmani* one, because Ahsan Shah, its founder, took the name also of the former master, Gangu Bahman, who had been kind to him when he started life in Delhi. This Bahmani kingdom lasted a long time, and at one period extended itself beyond the bounds given above. But like all eastern kingdoms its success only preceded its ruin. The dynasty lasted for

Plate V.

Coins of Babar, Humayun, Akbar and the Suris.

nearly two centuries, but finally was split up into kingdoms which had their capitals at Bijapur, Junair, and Ahmadnagar, Elichpur, Golconda, and Bidar. The Bahmani dynasty is represented by eighteen kings, who coined in the usual three metals. No known collection contains coins of all these kings. The British Museum collection begins with coins of the eighth king. There has never been any one keen on coins in the parts where the Bahmani kings ruled. The late Hon'ble James Gibbs made a collection of gold and silver coins of this dynasty during a time of famine. Captain Tufnell made a most interesting collection of coins of this part, issued it would seem by independent rulers, some of whom are noticed by Ibn-i-Batuta in his travels, but some are of men who are not mentioned in any history. From this collection it would seem that Muhammad Tuglaq had a special coinage for the Dekkan. Before this collection was published we knew of only one coin struck at Sultanpur, as Warangal, the capital of Telinga, was called, and of some struck at Deogir, or Dowlatabad as Muhammad Tuglaq re-named it. The history of Dekkan numismatics shows that a collector of coins for the whole country should be set to work. The Bahmani coins are interesting, not only because they have on them the names of the kings, but because of the small sentences in Arabic which they contain. They are all of superior workmanship, and thus show that the State which caused them to be struck was one of strength sufficient to produce a feeling of security.

Malwa seceded from the empire about the year 1400 *A. D.* Seven kings of two dynasties ruled over this country for about a century and a half. Of these the coins of five only are known. A goodly number of the coins are square, not only in gold, but in silver and copper. The copper coins are not rare, but a good one is seldom met with. The silver coins are exceedingly rare, but the gold coins are not unfrequently found. There is no good collection of Malwa coins as yet known. In the British Museum are only sixty-four.

Gujerat became independent of Delhi in 1396 *A. D.* It was nearly two centuries after this that Akbar re-conquered it and annexed it to his empire. During those two hundred years fourteen sovereigns ruled in this country, of whom the coins of eight only are at present known. From them it is evident that a trimetallic currency obtained in Gujerat. There is great variety in the inscriptions on the coins. No good collection has yet been made of these coins of Gujerat. Dr. DeCunha and Mr. Fardunjee of Bombay have some good specimens, but no one seems to have made an attempt to secure a good specimen of each type of each sovereign in each one of the three metals. Mr. E. E. Oliver three years ago wrote a very good paper on the coins of Gujerat and illustrated it with three plates. The British Museum catalogue contains figures of only ten coins.

Jaunpur threw off the yoke of Delhi in 1394, and it remained independent for nearly a century.

Six kings in all reigned during that one hundred years. The coins of two of these are known in gold, of only one in silver, and of four only in copper. The copper coins are of several types and sizes, and several sizes are dated in figures. A good deal of attention has been paid to these copper coins, as the British Museum has coins of nearly every year of each king who coined. Indeed the coins of the last king, Hussain Shah, must have been struck long after he left the country and even after his death. He fled to Bengal in 881 H. and died in 905 H.; but one series goes on without interruption up to 910 H. Bahlol Lodhi, who conquered Jaunpur, struck coins there in 888 and 889.

It is strange that while no copper coins have been found of any of the rulers in Bengal, the coins of Kulburga, Malwa, Gujerat, and Jaunpur are most frequently met with in copper. Great care must be exercised in assigning the coins of these four different provinces. Many of the names, such as Muhammad Mahmud, &c., are found in each series of coins. To avoid confusion the best way is to get the coins of the four series on a table and compare them. It will then be found that each series has a morphology of its own. When experienced numismatists, such as those employed in the British Museum, make mistakes, amateurs cannot be too careful. The coins of Bengal, Kashmir, the Dekkan, Malwa, Gujerat, and Jaunpur, as in the British Museum, are given in a large volume of the British Museum catalogues—"the Mahomedan States." A study of that volume shows how little has been done yet for the numismatics of the Indian empire. In India no officer has been set apart as yet to attend to this branch of archæology. The Coin Department in the British Museum has a regular staff of men over it, and it is to their labours we look for regular catalogues of Indian coins. These catalogues, while showing what has been done and what coins acquired, show that there is much yet to be done if the Indian Museum in Calcutta is ever to have a collection of coins worthy of the Indian empire.

Before commencing a description of the coins of the Moguls, it is necessary that we should anticipate matters somewhat. Babar, the first Mogul emperor of India, conquered the country in 1526 *A.D.* and died in 1531 *A.D.* His son, Humayun, succeeded him, but after a short reign of about eight years he was driven out of the country by an Afghan, Sher Shah Sur. Humayun became a wanderer in Sind, Afghanistan, Persia and Turkistan, and did not regain the throne of India for sixteen years, in 1554 *A. D.* Sher Shah and his descendants, Islam Shah, Muhammad Shah, Sikandar Shah, and Ibrahim Shah ruled India or quarrelled about it during those sixteen years. Sher Shah was a genius in his way. He saw that the coinage of former days would never do. It was impossible for any revenue accounts to be made up with coins of varying values, and we have seen that the coins of Feroz Tuglaq and of Bahlol and Sikandar Lodhi were of billon, a mixture of silver and copper, in which the silver varied very much. The gold and silver coins also varied in size and weight. He therefore determined to introduce a new gold, silver, and copper coinage. Of the gold coins few are known. The silver coins are not unfrequently met with. We ourselves had several rupees of each year. There are broad pieces with the king's name on them in Arabic and Hindi on one side, together with name of mint and date. They must have weighed about 180 grains when issued. No parts of the rupee are known in silver. They are fine coins, and a complete collection of them makes a good show, as the inscriptions vary very much, being sometimes in circles and sometimes in squares. He coined in several places,—Sharifabad, Delhi, Jahanpanah (a part of old Delhi), Shergarh, Agra, Gwalior, Chounsa, and Kalpi. This was another innovation. The greatest change, however, was in the copper coins. He commenced in his second year striking large coins in copper, weighing about 320 grains. These varied from three-quarters of an inch to a little over an inch in diameter, and they were in consequence very thick. In order that they might be available to the masses, he struck them all over his dominions. Coins are known of the Delhi, Agra, Alwar, Hiran, Gwalior, Malot, Kalpi, Narnol, Sambhal, Biana, Lucknow, Shergarh, Abu, and Nau mints. They must have been struck in vast numbers. Thoy were probably called *dams*, and in them Akbar ordered all revenue accounts to be rendered, every village or town being assessed at so many dams, not at so many rupees. Forty dams went to a rupee. There were halves, quarters, eighths, and sixteenths of these dams struck for small transactions. Islam Shah, son of Sher Shah, went on coining as his father had done, but he seems to have coined very little gold, as only one of his gold coins is known. His copper coins are, even now, exceedingly numerous, but until lately not one was known with a mint name on it: now, however, coins in copper of the Malot, Kalpi, Kanauj or Shergarh, Narnol, and Shahgarh mints are known. Muhammad Shah reigned only a short time, but his coins in copper are very common and in great variety. His silver coins are rare and his gold ones unknown. Sikandar and Ibrahim were always fighting, and the coins of both are very rare. A few rupees of the former are known, but no gold and only one one-eighth of a dam. Of Ibrahim only one half-rupee is known, and his copper dams are as rare as those of Sikandar's. It will be seen from the above what a field the coins of the Suri dynasty afford to the collector. Should any one wish to secure numismatic fame, let him obtain gold coins of each of these five kings and a rupee of Ibrahim, together with half, quarter, eighth, and sixteenth parts of the dams of Ibrahim and Sikandar. That they have not yet been found is no argument against their not being in existence. Let it be remembered that no systematic research has yet been conducted for Indian coins. Now one thing is pretty certain about Indian coins, and it is this: no king ever seems to have called in the coins of his predecessors. To this day this is the case, and we may in an ordinary town obtain from a money-changer the coins of many kings as the result of a casual visit. We remember in days gone by visiting a town on the Sind, Punjab, and Delhi Railway. We worked in its bazaar the whole of a long hot afternoon in May, and at night when we came to study our acquisitions we found we were in possession of the coins of no less than 58 kings, and of these there were different types and sizes of several kings. If we return to our last paper and to the beginning of the present one, we shall see what a tremendously large field the numismatist has before him, omitting the coinage of the Moguls, of which more in our next. But, of course, all the coins we have described in former papers are obtainable in Indian bazaars, and besides these there are coins which have not yet been brought to light. All these coins help to illustrate history and in many cases to make it. The historian of India cannot afford to neglect the study of coins; if he does, his history will be incomplete. Just now great attention is being paid to the history of India, and attempts are being made to fill up some of the gaps in it. It is only from coins and inscriptions that this can be done. Hitherto private enterprise has had the field to itself. It may be, however, that when the paucity of coins in our museums is known, an agent will be appointed to search all the bazaars of India for the historical treasures they contain. This is not a wild idea, but one based on experience. The Indian Museum has its natural history collectors at work both on land and sea, and the result is that the natural history section of that museum is one of the wonders of India. Hitherto the archæological section has depended on gifts and odd finds. It is now, however, regarded as an axiom with respect to collections, that if we want a collection to be really good, we must set up a standard and work away at collecting systematically and scientifically until we have attained that standard. Gifts may pour in. They may be and will be mostly of poor duplicates of things already possessed. We cannot afford to give them space. We want the best specimens of every type and species that constant, patient, long-continued research can procure.

XIII.

BEFORE Babar conquered India by defeating Ibrahim Lodhi on the field of Panipat, he had been a ruler for many years, and in various parts of Turkistan had issued coins in his own name. These coins were thin silver pieces which followed the fashion of the coins of the descendants of Taimur. It is evident, however, from the coins we havè of Babar, that he not only coined when he was settled in towns for a short period, but that he carried his mint along with him, and when encamped long enough at a place he ordered coins to be struck, and as the place had no name worthy of being made known to people, he simply ordered the word *Urdu*, or Camp, to be placed on his coins as the name of the mint. He never seems to have coined anything but silver before he came to India, as no copper or gold coins of his are known of the early, unsettled years of his life. Indeed no gold coin of his has yet been found, although it is known that Shah Ṛukh, the son of Taimur, struck small gold coins weighing a little over ten grains, and therefore equal in value to a rupee of the good old days. While Babar was in India he had a lively time of it. He found that Panipat was only a prelude to many such struggles, and the five years he lived as emperor of India were years of constant activity. Hence we often find his silver coins were struck in the Urdu, or Camp. On others the name of the town where he was staying comes, or it may be that regular mints were established in certain towns. Kabul, Jaunpur, Agra, and Lahore come oftenest. The silver coins of Babar are, however, exceedingly rare, and we need never expect to find many of them. In copper he seems to have struck only at one mint—Agra. Apparently this mint was located permanently at Agra, for the place is called *Dar-ul-Zarb, i. e.,* the mint. These copper coins have not Babar's name on them, but they have the year 936 H. on them and the name of the mint, so we know they were issued by Babar. They are in weight somewhat similar to the coins of Sikandar Lodhi. Some few coins are known on which Babar's name comes, struck over the name of the king who originally struck the coin, which was a fashion much in vogue in Turkistan amongst the descendants of Taimur.

Humayun, succeeding his father Babar, coined after the same style. As, however, several small gold coins of Humayun's are known, we may conjecture that in all probability Babar also coined in gold. The towns of Champanir, and Delhi, and Kandahar, in addition to those on Babar's coins, are mints coming on the thin silver coins of Humayun. Like his father, Humayun was fond of wine, and after he had conquered a place and the fight was over, nothing delighted him more than a party in a garden. At such times he could not feel angry with any one. Champanir is a town situated on a steep and almost precipitous rock, about forty miles north-east of Baroda. When Humayun, in the fifth year of his reign, sat before it to besiege it he found it was harder to take than he expected. One day he saw some grass-cutters coming from the jungle with their tattoos laden with forage. He watched them, and saw that they went to a part of the besieged town where the rock was nearly perpendicular. Ropes were let down from above, the loads of grass were attached to them, and were soon pulled up into the fort. Humayun returned to his camp and ordered long iron nails to be made, and a few nights afterwards he himself acting as leader, struck these nails one above the other into the rock until he had formed a ladder up which the army could mount the most inaccessible part of the citadel. Of course the place was taken, but the treasure which was known to be in the place could not be found. Some of Humayun's courtiers advised that the officer who had held the fort should be tortured: the counsels of others, who said that they had better have a feast and ply the officer with wine, prevailed. The feast was given, the sparkling goblet was circulated, and of course it came out that the treasure was all thrown into a tank. On the proceeds of that treasure Humayun went in for a big carouse. He did not neglect business; he ordered coins to be struck in Champanir which he called *Shahr-i-Mukarram*, the "liberal, generous or august city." He also called Jaunpur the mint of tne *blessed* district (*Mutabarrak* is the word used). Agra he called on his coins the *Gate of Safety*, "Dar-ul-Aman," or *Seat of Justice*, "Dar-ul-Adl." Delhi was called "Dar-ul-Mulk," *The Capital*. Lahore and Agra both rejoiced in the title of "Dar-ul-Khilafat," *The Seat of the Head of Religion*.

Humayun was personally brave, but he was no general. Sher Shah Sur inveigled him down to Bengal just before the rains set in, and then when the rains commenced left him and his army to the Bengal climate for a while. The result was that Humayun was driven from Bengal, defeated at Kanauj, expelled from Agra, pursued to Delhi, and at last was compelled to fly by way of Lahore and Multan to Sind. At Bhakkar he saw a beautiful girl named Hamida at a marriage feast. He at once married her, and she accompanied her husband in all his wanderings, giving birth to Akbar at Amarkote in Sind. Thence Humayun fled to Kandahar, and from that to Persia, where Tahmasp ruled. After some long time he obtained help from Tahmasp, returned and took Kandahar and Kabul. He spent some years between Kabul and Badakshan, and finally, after sixteen years of absence from India, he returned to this country to find the Suri family fighting amongst themselves. He defeated Sikandar Sur at Sirhind, and thus regained the empire of India. His son Akbar was then a boy of thirteen, and was declared the victor of Sirhind. Humayun did not live long after his return. He fell down a flight of stairs in a place he used as library in the old fort of Delhi. He lived long enough, however, to coin, and, strange to say, the only coin known of his after his return is a rupee in weight equal to those issued by Sher Shah. His death made the boy Akbar emperor of India, or rather of that part of India which had been reconquered by Humayun. We cannot, however, leave Humayun's coins just yet. He had a brother Kamran, who was a thorough Oriental. This brother was made governor of Kabul, and of course ruled there on his own account, and struck coins, therefore, in his own name. He coined in both Kabul and Kandahar, and did not hesitate to re-strike the coins of Humayun, putting his own name over that of his brother's. Kamran's story is a long one and a sad one. We cannot go into details, however, here. The coins of Humayun are very rare in silver, though exceedingly common in copper. In gold not a dozen are known. There is one little matter about some of Humayun's silver coins which ought to be noticed. On the reverse he added to the Mahomedan confession of faith—"Allah gives daily food, without account, to whom he will." It is from the last part of verse 211 of Chapter II of the Koran. This verse gives the key perhaps to the whole life of Humayun, which was one of utter carelessness and piety.

We now come to Akbar and his coins. Akbar was as near as possible a contemporary of our Queen Elizabeth. He reigned from 1556 to 1605

A.D., and died in the 50th year of his reign. We have proof that the reforms carried out in the coinage by Sher Shah were acceptable to the people of India in the fact that, although a few thin silver and small gold coins of Akbar are known, similar to those issued by his father Humayun, the great mass of Akbar's coins are rupees, or parts of rupees, mohurs, the same weight as rupees, and dams, the same weight as those issued by Sher Shah. The rupees and mohurs had on one side Akbar's name and titles, the year of the Hijira, and the name of the mint. On the reverse was the Kalima, together with names of the four companions of Muhammad and their titles or qualities. Delhi, Agra, and Lahore were the first great mints, but in time mints were established all over the country, until towards the end of Akbar's reign, when many provinces of India had been conquered and annexed, the mints show the full extent of Akbar's power. As the places are well known we may as well give the names of the mints on Akbar's coins, in order that the extent of his empire may be grasped :—Lahore, Agra, Delhi, Jaunpur, Fatehpur (Sikri ,near Agra), Patna, Oojain, Ahmedabad, Illahabad or Allahabad, Ulwar, Attock, Kabul, Ajmere, Chitur, Bhakkar, Hissar, Sirhind, Saharanpur, Gorakpur, Gobindpur, Bairat, Kalpi, Gwalior, Kanauj, Srinagar and Kashmir, Lucknow, Multan, Dogam, Burhānpur, Asirgarh, Taṭṭa in Sind, Lahri Bandar in Sind, Sitapur, a town in the district of Muzaffargarh in the Punjab, Udipur, Surat, Narnol, Malpur, Khairpur, and Urdu Zafar Qarin or the Victorious Camp,—forty mints in all. There are others given in the *Ain-i-Akbari*, and more yet may be discovered. For the first thirty years of Akbar's life his coinage shows but little change; a few alterations in the disposition of the parts of the inscriptions. One change, however, he introduced—square rupees and mohurs, probably in imitation of the coinage of Malwa. The rupee was divided into parts—halves, fourths, fifths, eighths, tenths, sixteenths and twentieths. The mohurs also were similarly divided, but there were gold coins of which no one specimen has come down to us. There were the one hundred gold-mohur piece and its divisions—halves, quarters, fifths, &c.

In the thirtieth year of Akbar's reign a change, which had long been coming on, showed itself in Akbar and his coins. He was always fond of religious discussions, and the result of all this was that he determined to found a new religion, with himself as god or object of worship. This, of course, caused him to throw over the Kalima and to invent a creed of his own. It was a short one اکبر الله جل جلاله It was never stamped with vowel marks, and so folks could please themselves how they read it. It may be interpreted "*God is the greatest, may his brightness shine forth,*" or "*Akbar is God,*" &c. There can be no doubt that Akbar intended the last meaning, and that he caused a new kind of salaam to be made to him when people approached him. He left off dating his coins in the Hijri year, and dated them from the first year of his own reign. Thus changing his coins in his 30th year, he called it the "*Divine*" year 30. If his year were divine how much more so his person. This was what he intended to convey to the minds of people who read and understood his coins. As his mints were at work all the year, he determined to make his rupture with Mahomedanism more perfect, and so he discarded the use of the Arabian months and used the names of the months as they were known to the old fire worshippers of Persia. On one side of the rupee therefore we see Akbar's creed and on the other the divine year, the month, and the name of the mint. The gold coinage after the 30th year followed the same fashion. So did the copper. But with the copper came other changes. On the early copper the name of the coin was put *fulus*, or *sikka*; on the divine year coinage we get *tanka*, *half tanka*, *quarter tanka*, *eighth part of a tanka*, *and sixteenth part of a tanka*. The weight of a tanka was equal to that of two dams, or over 640 grains. The word *dam* never comes on any coin, but on one coin is the word *nim dam*, *i. e.*, half-a-dam. On one coin, too, comes the word *nisfe*, a half. There are coinlike pieces which were issued from Akbar's mints as one, two or four "*tanke*" pieces. These are not tankas but *weights*. The *Ain-i-Akbari* tells us there were other weights issued; they are exactly like coins having the mint, month, divine year, and Akbar's creed on them, just as the rupees and copper coins have.

The coins that are known do not tally exactly with the description of the coins given in the *Ain-i-Akbari*. We have no large gold coins in our museums, and consequently we cannot say whether these large coins had on them the poetry said to have been stamped on them. On one known mohur of Akbar's and on one rupee we have a Persian couplet. The mohur was struck at Agra and the rupee at Allahabad. These Persian couplet mohurs adhered to the divine year and the old Persian months. They were the precursors of many of the same kind struck by the son of Akbar, the well-known Jahangir. On one gold mohur struck at Asir (garh) there was a hawk on one side, standing in the middle of a scroll with leaves and flowers. The other side recorded the creed, mint, month, and divine year. On another mohur were images of Sita and Ram, with their names in Sanskrit. It is from this coin that all coins with images on them are named "*Sita-Rami*" by modern coin dealers.

There is one mohur, and only one known, struck at Udipur. On it is written that it was struck at *Muhammadabad*, known as Udipur, the *conquered*. How different was the conduct of Humayun at Champanir, the *generous august* city. Akbar's success spoiled him and made him a snob.

The collector will see that Akbar's coins afford a good field for his energies. First of all, he *may* get a rupee of each year. Then he may get all the parts of the rupee. Then he may get a rupee from every mint that struck them. Then he may try for one rupee of each month of one mint, and after that he can get a rupee of each year and of each month of each year and of each mint. The gold coins offer the same field. The copper are still numerous in our bazaars. So first of all let the collector try for a dam of each of Akbar's fifty years; then let him try to collect copper from every mint. Then let him get tankas and halves, &c., from every mint. If he likes he can try for the months of every year of every mint. He will need money to start with and several cabinets for his acquisitions. There is no knowing what he might find. He might by chance obtain one of those quaint mohurs of Akbar's which we have omitted to describe. It was neither round nor square but oblong, and the ends were not straight, but had in their middle a projection like a Gothic arch. These were from the Agra mint and were of both types, with the Kalima, and with Akbar's creed, month and divine year. One edited by Mr. Delmerick is dated 981, ten years before Akbar s change in religion was declared. It has on it Akbar's creed, and instead of mint or month the words "Oh! unchangeable one" یامعین This form of mohur is very rare indeed.

And now one word about forgeries and imitations. The rupees and mohurs have the Kalima on them and the four companions' names. These are very precious to some Musalmans. Coins possessing them are, therefore, in great request, and sell for more than their intrinsic value. Some four years ago the bazaars of Northern India were deluged with square rupees purporting to have been struck in Lahore in 988 H. Anyone who could read could see that the inscriptions were full of mistakes. We saw a gold mohur of this kind which had been secured by an officer in Kabul, and got no thanks from him for pointing out that it was an impudent attempt at imitation. The other day we came across an eight-anna piece with Akbar's early camp mint on one side and Ranjit Singh's Amritsar stamp on the other. In this case the Amritsar mint authorities must have acquired an old die of Akbar's camp mint and used it. When we consider the number of mints at work, we are astonished more forgeries do not exist. When we consider that these mints were in remote parts of the empire, we are astonished that the coinage was so uniform with respect to weight and purity of metal, and we sit down from an examination of Akbar's coinage with the conviction that the subjects of Akbar were down-right honest men, who worked in remote places just as fairly as they did under the immediate superintendence and presence of the emperor. There must have been in a man who could thus rule something akin to what Her Most Gracious Majesty our own Queen-Empress possesses so amazingly—the power of creating loyalty. No other king of India was ever served as was Akbar. No other ruler in any country or any age was ever so loyally served as has been and still is the Queen-Empress Victoria.

XIV.

WE have in the Ain-i-Akbari an account of Akbar's mint, or rather mints. That account is meagre in the extreme, and the coins themselves, as found at the present day in the bazaars of Indian towns, give us, as we have seen, much more complete data for compiling a full story of Akbar's coinage. The coins said to have been issued by Jahangir are described in the Tozuk-i-Jahangiri It may be that the coins therein described were actually issued; if so, they have not come down to us, but many coins are now in existence which certainly bear Jahangir's name, but are not described in Jahangir's biography. He gives the names of gold and silver coins which were 100 tolas each, and 50 and 20 and 10 and 5. These were all equal in weight to 100, &c., mohurs or rupees. None of these have come down to us. In the course of his work he tells us that he gave as a present a gold coin worth Rs. 6,400, or say, a 400-mohur piece. In another place he bestowed a mohur of 500 tolas on Adil Khan. There were coins in both gold and silver, both square and round, a tola-and-a-quarter in weight. These the emperor does not notice. The chief feature of Jahangir's coinage is the Persian couplets struck on the coins. Of these couplets Jahangir gives but a few: the coins, however, supply us with nearly forty. These couplets, though ingenious, are pure rubbish; full of stupid flattery. Jahangir's first issues were orthodox: they had on one side the Kalima, and on the other Jahangir's name and title, together with the mint and year. About his fifth year he adopted the method of his father Akbar and used the divine year (thus deifying himself) and the old Persian months. He never returned to the Kalima. In Sir Thomas Roe's journal we have amusing accounts of Jahangir and his court. The emperor was very fond of his cups and of religious discussions. He invariably had recourse to the cups first: the discussions followed, and after that the king would weep and desire to be assisted to bed. On some rare gold mohurs he is represented as sitting on his throne with a wine cup in his hand. On the reverse is the sun, and a couplet to the effect that the numerical value of the letters in his own name and that of God is the same. The most beautiful series of the coins of Jahangir are his zodiacal mohurs and rupees. These have on one side one of the signs of the zodiac, and on the other a Persian couplet. They were struck at Ahmedabad and Agra, but one is known from the Fatehpur Sikri mint. On the real coins the lion, or bull, or crab is represented in the middle of the sun. All the images are done with artistic grace and accuracy. It is supposed they were the work of some Italian artist. They form a beautiful and unique series of Indian coins, but they are very scarce, and copies and forgeries are known of the whole set. Jahangir was the first to coin *nisars* or coins for scattering among the people on birthdays and coronation anniversaries. Strange to say these coins, which must have been thrown away by the thousand, are now seldom met with. They are of exquisite workmanship, and weigh about the same as a four-anna piece. There is one mohur and one rupee we must not omit to mention; the ones which bear the names of Jahangir and Nur Jahan, his beautiful and favourite sultana. This is the only name of a queen consort which is found on any purely Indian coin. Razia Begam was queen in her own right. Nur Jahan was empress of India *in fact* during the latter years of Jahangir. We do not give the couplets on Jahangir's coins or the couplet in which the names of Jahangir and Nur Jahan came. Any one desirous of studying the poetry on these coins is referred to the *journal* of the Asiatic Society of Bengal for 1888, or to the *Calcutta Review* of October, 1891, where all are given with translations.

The copper coins of Jahangir are exceedingly rare; some are stamped on the Suri coins. Copper coins were not wanted in his time. The bazaars were deluged with the daṃs of the Suri dynasty and with the copper coinage of Akbar, who had kept his mints at work for 50 years. If the revenue was paid in dams as well as assessed in the same coins, they must have been

Plate VI.

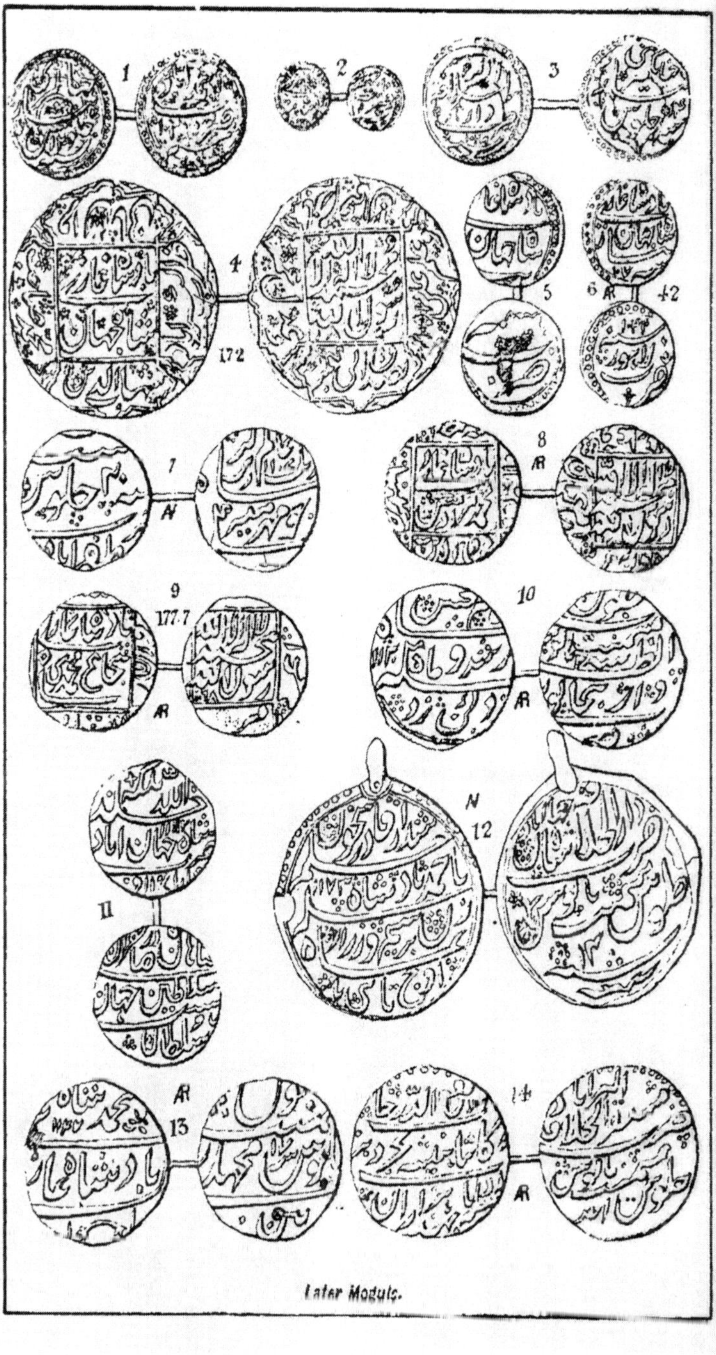

Later Moguls.

exceedingly numerous. It is pretty certain that the army was paid in dams even in the time of Jahangir.

Jahangir's successor was Shah Jahan, the builder of the Taj at Agra and of modern Delhi, which, after him, is known amongst Muhammadans as Shahjahanabad. His coins in gold and silver revert to the use of the Kalima on the reverse. But so used had the people got to the Persian months and the divine year that one series of his coins has both the Kalima and the divine year and the Persian month on them. He left off the use of poetry, too, on his coins. The only interest indeed which his coins possess is the names of the mints on them. These show the extent of his empire. His copper coins are exceedingly rare.

Aurangzeb, the son of Shah Jahan, reigned nearly 51 lunar years. He was a strict Musalman, and from the commencement of his reign forbad the use of the Kalima on his coins, giving as a reason his objection to seeing so holy a thing as the profession of faith in the hands of an infidel. As he did not call in the rupees of his father or great-grandfather, of course they still handled such coin. He invented a couplet of his own, and he adhered to it all through his long reign, so that his coin inscriptions are monotonous in the extreme. One deviation seems to have taken place, but that was only in the name and title of the king. His mints are very numerous, and this gives his coins some interest. In his days the Mogul empire reached its greatest extent, and in his days the disintegration of the empire set in, so that a complete set of the years and mints of this emperor shows the full extent of the empire, and also tells us when certain provinces ceased to acknowledge Aurangzeb as their suzerain. Rupees are obtainable of all the years of Aurangzeb, and from about fifty mints. After Aurangzeb the coins of the emperors began to show signs of carelessness. They give us, as a rule, the names of the kings and little else. Shah Alam I. reigned only five years, Jahander Shah part of one, Farrukh Siyar over seven. The two latter had couplets on their coins. In the same year that Farrukh Siyar died, three kings ascended the throne, Rafia-ud Darajat, Shah Jahan II., and Muhammad Shah, the two first of whom reigned only a few months each. Muhammad Shah reigned thirty-one years. It was in his time that Nadir Shah invaded India and got as far as Delhi, which he plundered, taking away, amongst other things, the peacock throne. He stayed in Delhi about a month-and-a-half. His massacre of the inhabitants is well known. It is not so well known that he made his soldiers give up the plunder they had obtained in the city, and with it he caused rupees to be struck in Shahjahanabad. The rupees of Muhammad Shah show that the artists who cut the dies were a very low type of workmen. After Muhammad Shah, Ahmad Shah and Alamgir II. reigned, and it was during their times that the country was again overrun by Ahmad Shah,

Abdalli or Durrani, the successor of Nadir. The Durrani, like Babar, must have carried his mint along with him ; for wherever he went he struck coins. It was he who checked the growing power of the Sikhs, and who utterly defeated the Mahrattas at Panipat. Side by side and year by year the coins of the emperor of Delhi and of the Durrani invader were struck in Lahore and Delhi. In the intervals of the incursions of Ahmad, the Sikhs began to strike coins in Lahore. At last Shah Alam II. came to the throne, but the Punjab had gone out of the hands of the ruler of Delhi. The Sikhs coined in Lahore, Amritsar and Anandgarh. Only the small State of Jammu remained faithful to Delhi and coined rupees in the name of Shah Alam. On no other Punjab mint does his name come. The successors of the Durrani continued to strike coins when they were in power in Kashmir, Derajat, Multan and Peshawar. The successes of Ranjit Singh, however, soon stopped all this, and Sikh rupees were coined in all these places, as well as in Lahore, Amritsar, Pind Dadan Khan and other towns.

Shah Alam, blinded though he was, reigned in Delhi nearly 49 years. His power was very limited, but his name was used all over the country on coins. The East India Company struck millions of rupees in his name, and on them we have the names of Murshidabad, Benares, Farrukhabad and Surat, though the real mints were Calcutta and Bombay. These Company rupees are at once recognised by the excellence of their workmanship and by their uniformity. The year of each mint was fixed. They are therefore utterly useless to the historian. Not so, however, are those struck in native mints. These native mints were so numerous that they bred confusion, for each had different weights and different amounts of alloy in their rupees. The piece of metal struck was much smaller than the die, and hence only part of the inscription comes on the coin. Generally there was no room for the name of the mint. We know them, however, from the symbols used by the mints. The powers that struck them were often ephemeral, and the numbers of the coins issued were not great. The Company got possession of Delhi early in the present century. The empire of the Mogul was restricted to the Fort of Delhi. Three hundred years before that time an Alam Shah, or king of the world, had reigned in Delhi and its environs, and the wits had said of him that he was *Badshah-i-Alam az Delhi ta Palam*, *i. e.*, king of the world from Delhi to Palam, a town a short distance from the city. After Shah Alam, Akbar II. and Bahadur Shah were emperors in name, and they struck mohurs and rupees in the Fort of Delhi on birthdays and anniversaries, for distribution amongst their adherents. These are of necessity very rare, those of the mutineer, Bahadur Shah, being rarer than those of the first Moguls, Babar and Humayun. Native States, however, struck coins in the names of both Akbar II. and Bahadur Shah until the Mutiny.

But long before that time the Company's rupee had ceased to bear the name of Shah Alam, and to take instead the name of William IV. as King, and of Victoria as Queen. Native States, however, which had coined during the time of the fall of the Mogul empire, kept their mints going and keep them going now; some are adopting the standard of the rupee of the Empress, and others keep to a standard of their own. It would be a good thing to have a Currency Commission and reduce the whole of the coinage of India to one standard. In the Punjab, Kashmir and Pattiala only keep up their mints. The Kashmiri chilka rupee is worth only about ten annas, and the Pattiala one about fourteen. The Kashmiri coin bears on it the Christian letters I. H. S. We have heard that Maharaja Gulab Singh tried on his coins all kinds of signs, considering them powerful talismans. A renegade Native Christian, who had been taught English, sought refuge in Kashmir and obtained service under the Maharajá. He was asked what the most powerful talisman used by the Christians was. He at once bethought him of the letters which meet the eye of everyone on entering a church—those on the Communion Table cloth. The Maharaja ordered them to be struck on his coins, and there they are to this day, though not a soul in Kashmir knows their meaning.

The coins of the East India Company can easily be studied by any one interested in the subject if he will visit any native bazaar. It presents many points of interest which will at once be evident. The chief features are of course the change of the king's name and then the assumption by Her Most Gracious Majesty of the title of Empress.

We had intended to write *in extenso* of the octagonal coins of Assam, with their Sanskrit inscriptions in Bengali letters, and of the thin, broad, silver coins of Nepal, with their Sanskrit inscriptions and Hindoo symbols. These two series of coins will be at once known, and the kings who struck them will be seen from a perusal of their inscriptions.

Two kinds of gold coins, worn commonly round the neck, demand a notice. They are either Dutch ducats or Bokhara tilas. Of the former, there must be millions in the country. They are known at once from the figure in armour on one side and the Latin inscription in a square on the other: the Bokhara tilas are the coins of the Amirs of Bokhara. They weigh about the same as a ducat. Some were struck at Khotan or Kashgir or Khiva. Merchants from Central Asia bring them into the country. Both these kinds of gold coins are purchased with avidity by the middle and poorer classes; they are made into necklets and are sported on festive occasions. They serve two purposes—they are ornaments and at the same time accumulated wealth.

Foreign coins of all kinds come to India. To write of them would be to write of the coinage of the whole world. We have already trespassed too far on the patience of our readers. We trust that we have shown them that Indian numismatics may be made an interesting study, and that the hoards in the bazaars of Indian towns may be the source whence many an interesting problem may be obtained. Let it be remembered that every coin was struck by somebody, in some place, and at some time, and every piece of metal becomes at once a teacher of history, geography and chronology.

SUPPLEMENTARY LETTER.

SOUTH of the Sutledge is the large state of Pattiala. The great Ahmad Shah Durrani created the first Maharaja of this state. In gratitude the Maharaja used the Persian coin couplet of the Durrani. All the Maharajas of Pattiala have used the same couplet on their gold and silver coins, and have never caused their own names to be stamped on their coins. Different Maharajas have used different signs, and it is by these that the coins are assigned to those who struck them. The rupees are, in size, about as broad as a four-anna piece, but very thick and dumpy. As the couplet requires a goodly amount of space, only a part of it comes on the coin. One strange thing is noteworthy. The mint is in Pattiala city, but the name of the mint coming on the coin is *Sarhind* or *Sahrind* (سهرند), a town famous as a mint of the Mogul Emperors of India from the time of Akbar. When, however, we consider that the Maharaja is a Sikh, and that the Sikhs account Sarhind accursed, because two of the sons of their last Guru were slain in this town, the retention of the name seems stranger still. Ahmad Shah Durrani coined in this town, and that is perhaps the reason its name is retained on Pattiala coins.

Maler Kotla, Jind, and Nabha are three other states near Pattiala. These all coined similarly to Pattiala, but Maler Kotla being a Muhammadan state, used no signs: instead of them the initial letters of the names of the rulers were placed on the coins. Jind and Nabha used the old Sikh couplet on their coins, instead of the Durrani one. This Sikh coin couplet is found on the early Sikh rupees. I have already mentioned something about the Sikh coins, but I have not stated that the earliest Sikh rupees were struck at Lahore in 1765 A. D. The Sikhs were then 12 misls of freebooters. Two or three of these misls held Lahore in 1765, and coined there. Eight years afterwards they began to coin in Amritsar. Ranjit Singh did not get possession of Lahore till 1800 A. D. Rupees coined in that city by the Sikhs as a community may still be obtained for each of the 35 years preceding his time. Ranjit Singh never put his name on a coin, but an infamous woman, who obtained great influence over him, one Mora ("Mora" means a peacock) put her mark, a peacock's tail, on rupees and mohurs issued from the Amritsar mint. The mints of Ranjit Singh must have been busy during the whole of his long reign, for his coins in gold, silver and copper are still numerous. It is strange that so few Sikh coins are found with Gurmukhi characters on them The majority of the Sikh coins have Persian inscriptions.

Bahawulpur is a large and important state, south of the western part of the Sutledge. It had three mint towns of its own—Bahawulpur,

Ahmadpur, and Khairpur These issued silver coins. Small copper coins with a thorn branch on them with no mint name were struck in Bahawulpur. Even now small square copper coins with a crescent and a star and the thorn branch on one side and the name of the town on the other are being struck for change. Mahmud Shah Durrani coined double mohurs at Bahawulpur: they are about the finest and rarest of modern Indian coins.

I have hitherto said but little about the coins of the Durrani family who succeeded the great Ahmad Shah of Panipat celebrity. His last incursion into the Punjab was not a success: he had to retrace his steps somewhat ignominiously. His son Taimur Shah never had a chance in the Punjab after his father's death. He continued to hold the Trans-Indus provinces, and his coins struck at Bhakhar, Derajat and Peshawar are not scarce in either gold or silver or copper. But no Lahore coin of his is known after he became king; his Kashmir coins, however, are common. The Durranis had always to fight for their thrones; they had to fight to get them; they had to fight to keep them; often the throne of Kabul had no occupant. The mint, always at work, at such times struck coins in the name of "The Man of the Time." A complete collection of the rupees and coins of the Trans-Indus provinces and of Afghanistan, since the commencement of the present century, would give us the names and the date and the possessions of all the rulers who have held sway in that part of the world. The rupees and mohurs are not things of beauty: they are rough pieces, of metal, and no *one* coin has ever the whole inscription on it. The new rupees of the present Amir are well struck by machinery. Let us hope they are the precursors of a general civilisation for Afghanistan.

Kabul, Kandahar and Herat have had mints at work for hundreds of years. The copper coins struck there are very numerous : most of them have only the dates and mint names on them. They occupy therefore the same position as the copper tokens of our own land. Old autonomous coins of this type are now seldom met with, but new Kandahar coins are very common. The devices on them are numerous and exceedingly varied.

In a heap of common bazaar coins in the northern towns of India at the present day coins of Bhopal, Baroda, Gwalior, Indore, Amritsar, Lahore, Jummu and Srinagar (Kashmir) are the most common. But there is always a vast number of copper coins, the origin of which the coin-dealers can tell us but little about. The Mansuri pice are coins of this kind. They are as a rule, oblong lumps of copper or brass. They are without inscriptions, and have generally no devices on them. Of course, they are not of equal weights. In some bazaars remote from trade routes I have seen shapeless lumps of iron or copper or mixed metal sold for coin. Strange though it may seem, these coins are in great demand. When a marriage takes place it is the custom to distribute coins to faqirs and the poor. Over a hundred of the pice above described are obtainable for a rupee, whereas only 64 pice stamped in Government mints can be got for the same sum. Hence it happens that the common bazaar money-changer does a great trade in the old copper issues of the country. He buys up from villages and towns the money given away at marriages, &c., and in the marrying season drives a roaring trade in selling the same coins again. The coin collector looks on with approbation: he knows that from the villages along with this old coin will come others that have been found in the fields, &c., and this knowledge urges him to keep on visiting the money-changer, who from every purchase carefully selects coins not in the issues needed for alms-giving.

Petty principalities often supply many coins. There is a small province in the Himalayas which is called Garhwal. Its capital was Srinagar. A hundred years or so ago it had a Maharaja named Pardoman Shah. This man's coins are most plentiful. I saw a collection of copper rubbish once in Calcutta; and there were several of his coins in it. I scarcely ever examine a heap of copper in a bazaar of Northern India without coming across a lot of his coins.

Again, Nahan is the capital of the small hill state of Sirmoor, a few miles east of Kalka. Some years ago I came across a copper coin struck at this town. Its inscriptions told me that it was struck in 1812 A. D. It had on it two names—one the name of the Maharaja Judhbir and the other that of his servant Bahadur Shah. After some search I ascertained that in 1812 the Gurkhas held possession of Sirmoor, and that the general stationed there was Bahadur Shah. The Maharaja was Judhbir of Nepal. Such a coin was a whole chapter of condensed history.

The Sikhs in some of their predatory excursions went as far as the Duab between the Ganges and Jumna. It is not astonishing then that there are coins in existence on one side of which is the old Sikh coin distich and on the other the Najibabad mint name and mark. One coin of this kind is known with the Jaipur mint name and mark, though I do not recollect reading anywhere that the Sikhs ever held that city. Sir Henry Lawrence told us in his "Adventures of an Officer in the Punjab" that the Sikhs were given to bragging. This Sikh Jaipur coin is not by any means the first instance of bragging on coins. I remember seeing years ago a coin struck at Surat with the Sikh coin couplet on it, and it is certain the Sikhs never held Surat. The Sikh coiners were not at all particular. I had a coin, a square 8-anna piece; it had on one side the Sikh leaf and on the other the Urdu Zafar Qarin inscription of Akbar, with year *alif*, or one thousand.

We should not expect to find modern coins from remote countries in Northern India. But nevertheless many are found. Pilgrims from Mecca and Medina bring the coins of the Turkish empire. Punjab policemen from Hongkong bring Chinese dollars and copper coins of the new North Borneo Trading Company, and the coins in use in the Straits Settlements. The same men must have brought Mexican coin and coins from Hawaii and the Sandwich islands. Punjabis must also have brought coins from Zanzibar and the Mauritius. Persian merchants are responsible for modern Persian coins as are the Kashgar traders for the coins of Turkistan and the extreme western provinces of China. But who brought Lima shillings of George III. and his crowns? And who brought all the many English tokens we meet with? And who spread abroad advertisements in the shape of coins? Surely Professor Holloway and his pills and ointment were well known enough not to need the fictitious aid of coins. The Professor did not think so. He had his bust struck on one side together with his name, and on the other the advertisement of his medicines. These are not the only extravagances we meet with in coins. A Governor-General once sent an Agent of the name of Bushby to Jhansi. The Raja of that state at once ordered a coin to be struck in his name: one side is occupied with "AGENT BUSHBY SAHEB," and the other has a Persian inscription surrounding a lion so attenuated that it looks like a half-starved London tom-cat. From all this it is evident that the coin collector in Northern India should always keep a space for out-of-the-way things.

Medals are allied to coins. In the whole of my experience I have met with only one war medal which shows that what is hardly won is duly appreciated by the winners and their heirs.

Only one of the many satraps who have ruled provinces of India ever had the cheek to put his bust on a medal. This was a ruler who prided himself on his likeness to Napoleon the Third. He held an exhibition in his province, and had a medal struck in honour of himself and the event. I have only met with two of these in thirty years. Let us hope they are all melted down.

There were medals struck in honour of General Claude Martin, the founder of the Martinière Schools. They are in copper in two sizes. One side has the General's bust and motto: the other has a Persian inscription with his title.

One medal I had presented to me by the late Viceroy and Governor-General of India, the Marquiss of Dufferin and Ava, who was interested in my numismatic researches, and who is himself no mean archæologist.

One coin I have not yet been able to find. George Thomas was the only Irishman who ever became a raja in India by the right of conquest. His capital was Hissar, which he called Georgegarh. In his biography his own words are quoted, in which he says: "I coined rupees in my own name." He died ninety years ago, and as yet no one has found one of his coins.

There are many common coins which have not been assigned to any place or person. There is no information obtainable in the bazaars, and the coins themselves supply none. They seem to have been struck to supply change. Besides these there are many coins on which are signs or portions of words which mark them as local issues, but their locality is now forgotten. These coins must always be of the lowest historical value. From what we have said, however, it is evident that the Punjab and Northern India supply so many different series of coins that the numismatist must of necessity content himself with studying only a few of them. Should he wish to master the whole, he must give himself years of leisure—and I do not know that pleasure could be prolonged in any other study through so many years of discovery. This it is which gives zest to the study of the coins of Northern India,—constant discovery of new coins which throw light on an imperfectly written and little known history of a constantly changing series of dynasties.

BOOKS ON THE COINS OF NORTHERN INDIA.

(1) Marsden's Numismata Orientalia, London, 1825. 57 plates. Plates only. Trübner & Co., London, 1869.

(2) Plates at end of Burne's Travels.

(3) Wilson's Ariana Antiqua, London, 1841. 22 plates.

(4) Masson's Travels, Vol. III, chap. 7.

(5) Prinsep's Indian Antiquities, edited by Thomas. Many plates.

(6) Lieutenant Cunningham on Bactrian Coins. J. A. S. B. 1840. 1 plate.

(7) Lieutenant Cunningham : 2nd notice of some new Bactrian Coins. 1842. 1 plate.

(8) Lieutenant Cunningham : some unpublished Indo-Scythian Coins. 1845. 1 plate.

(9) Major Cunningham : Coins of Indian Buddhist Satraps. 1854. 2 plates.

(10) Edward Thomas on the Coins of the Gupta Dynasty. 1855.

(11) Edward Thomas : Ancient Indian Weights. 1865.

(12) Major-General Cunningham's Coins of the Nine Nagas and of two other Dynasties of Narwar and Gwalior. 1865. 1 plate.

(13) Points in the History of the Greek and Indo-Scythian Kings in Bactria, Kabul and India, by Roeer and Torrens from Lassen.

(14) The Initial Coinage of Bengal, by Edward Thomas. 2 plates and cuts. 1867.

(15) The Early Faith of Asoka, by Edward Thomas. 1877. 2 plates of coins.

(16) The Identity of Xandrames and Krananda, by Edward Thomas. 1877.

(17) The Bilingual Coins of Bokhara, by Edward Thomas. 1877. 1 plate.

(18) Bactrian Coins, by Edward Thomas. 1877. 1 plate.

(19) On the Coins of the Kings of Ghazni, by Edward Thomas. 1847. 3 plates.

(20) Supplement to above, by Edward Thomas. 1859. 1 plate.

(21) On the Coins of the Hindu Kings of Kabul, by Edward Thomas. 1846. 1 plate.

(22) The Ancient Coinage of Kashmir, by Lieutenant A. Cunningham. 1843.

(23) Coins of the Successors of Alexander in the East, by Major-General A. Cunningham. 16 plates.

(24) Chronicles of the Pathan Kings of Delhi, by Edward Thomas. 6 plates and many cuts. London, Trübner & Co., 1871.

(25) Coins of the Indian Prince Sophytes, a contemporary of Alexander the Great, by Major-General Cunningham. 1 cut.

(26) Dates on the Coins of the Hindu Kings of Kabul, by Sir Edward Clive Bayley. 2 plates.

(27) Coins of the Arabs in Sind, by Edward Thomas. Indian Antiquary. Cuts.

(28) Gold and Silver Coins of the Bahmani Dynasty, by Hon. J. Gibbs. 1 plate.

(29) Some Rare and Unpublished Coins of the Pathan and Mogul Dynasties of Delhi, by Hon. J. Gibbs. 2 plates.

(30) Copper Coins of the Bahmani Dynasty, by Dr. Codrington. 1 plate.

(31) Coins of the Mitra or Sanga Dynasty, by H. Rivett-Carnac. 3 plates.

(32) Coins of the Kings of Delhi and Jaunpur, by J. G. Delmerick. 1 plate.

(33) Coins of the Kings of Delhi, Malwa, Bengal, Kulburga and Kashmir, by J. G. Delmerick. 1876. 2 plates.

(34) Description of Coins and Relics found by Mr. W. Simpson in the Ahin Posh Stupa, Jalalabad. 1879. 5 plates.

(35) Coins of Ghiyas-ud-din and Muizz-ud-din-bin Sam, by Dr. Stulpnagel. 1 plate.

(36) Coins of Khusrau Shah and Khusrau Malik and others. 1 plate. C. J Rodgers.

(37) Copper Coins of the Maharajas of Kashmir. 2 plates. C. J. Rodgers.

(38) Copper Coins of the Sultans of Kashmir. 1 plate. C. J. Rodgers.

(39) Square Silver Coins of Sultans of Kashmir. 3 plates. C. J. Rodgers.

(40) Coins of the Maharajas of Kangra. 1 plate. C. J. Rodgers.

(41) Coins Supplementary to Thomas's "Chronicles of Pathan Kings." 2 plates. C. J. Rodgers.

(42) 2nd Supplement to Thomas's "Chronicles of Pathan Kings." 2 plates. C. J. Rodgers.

(43) 3rd Supplement to Thomas's "Chronicles of Pathan Kings." 2 plates. C. J. Rodgers.

(44) 4th Supplement to Thomas's "Chronicles of Pathan Kings." 2 plates. C. J. Rodgers.

(45) 5th Supplement to Thomas's "Chronicles of Pathan Kings." (In preparation.) 2 plates. C. J. Rodgers.

(46) Copper Coins of Akbar. 2 plates. C. J. Rodgers.

(47) Some more copper coins of Akbar. 1 plate. C. J. Rodgers.

(48) Rare Copper Coins of Akbar. 2 plates. C. J. Rodgers.

(49) A Find of Coins, struck by Ghazni Sultans in Lahore. C. J. Rodgers.

(50) The Coins of the Sikhs. 5 plates. C. J. Rodgers.

(51) Miscellaneous Coins. 1 plate. C. J. Rodgers.

(52) Rupees of the Months of Akbar's Ilahi Years. 2 plates. C. J. Rodgers.

(53) Coins of Ahmad Shah Durrani, struck in India. 1 plate. C. J. Rodgers.

(54) Notes on Coins described by Major Raverty in his foot-notes to the Translation of the Tabaqat-i-Nasiri. C. J. Rodgers.

(55) Some Coins from Kandahar. 1 plate. C. J. Rodgers.

(56) Coins of Nadir Shah, struck in India. 1 plate. C. J. Rodgers.

(57) Coins of Shams-ud-din Mahmud Shah. 1 cut. C. J. Rodgers.

(58) Notes on Nisars and Silver Coins of Aurangzeb. 1 plate. C. J. Rodgers.

(59) Couplets on the Coins of Jahangir. C. J. Rodgers.

(60) Couplets on Coins of Kings after Jahangir. C. J. Rodgers.

(61) Coins of Ranjit Deo, Raja of Jummu. 1 plate. C. J. Rodgers.

(62) Rupees of the Suri Dynasty. 2 plates. C. J. Rodgers.

(63) The Old Coins of the Punjab: a lecture. 3 plates. C. J. Rodgers.

(64) Catalogue of Coins in Lahore Museum. C. J. Rodgers.

(65) Catalogue of Coins in Indian Museum, Part I. The Sultans of Delhi and their Contemporaries. (In the press.) C. J. Rodgers.

(66) Catalogue of Mogul and Suri Coins collected by C. J. Rodgers and sold to Punjab Government. (In the press.) C. J. Rodgers.

(67) On a Silver Coin of Dawar Bakhsh. 1 cut. J. G. Delmerick.

(68) On a Gold Coin of Kam Bakhsh. 1 cut. J. G. Delmerick.

(69) Some Copper Coins of Akbar found in the Kangra District. 2 plates. E. E. Oliver.

(70) Decline of the Samanis and Rise of the Ghaznis. 3 plates. E. E. Oliver.

(71) Coins of the Muhammadan Kings of Gujarat. 3 plates. E. E. Oliver.

(72) Coins of the Chaghtai Moguls. 4 plates. E. E. Oliver.

(73) Coinage of the Early or Imperial Gupta Dynasty of Northern India. 5 plates. by Vincent Arthur Smith

(74) Observations on the Gupta Coinage. Vincent Arthur Smith. 2 plates.

(75) The Western Kshatrapas. 2 plates. By Pandit Bhagwanlal Indraji. Edited by E. J. Rapson.

(76) Notes on Historical Results deducible from recent discoveries in Afghanistan. 17 plates. H. T. Prinsep. 1844.

(77) Coins of the Indo-Scythians. 4 plates. Sir Alex. Cunningham.

(78) Coins of the Tochari, Kushans, or Yueti. Sir Alex. Cunningham. 1 plate.

(79) Coins of the Sakas. Sir Alex. Cunningham. 13 plates.

(80) Coins of the later Indo-Scythians. Sir Alex. Cunningham. 3 plates.

(81) New Coins of Bactria and India. Percy Gardner. 1 plate.

(82) Some New and Rare Muhammadan and Hindu Coins. Dr. Hoernle. 1 plate.

(83) Central Asian Coins collected by Captain Lassoe. Dr. Hoernle and C. J. Rodgers. 2 plates.

(84) Coins of the Durranis. M. Longworth Dames. 1 plate.

(15) The Epoch of the Sah Kings of Surashta. Edward Thomas.

(86) The Dynasty of the Guptas in India. Edward Thomas. 1 plate and cuts.

(87) Copper Coins of the Suri Dynasty. Dr. Hoernle. 3 plates.

(88) British Museum Catalogue: Oriental Coins, Vol. II. 8 plates.

(89) British Museum Catalogue: Greek and Scythian Kings. 32 plates.

(90) British Museum Catalogue: Sultans of Delhi. 9 plates.

(91) British Museum Catalogue: Muhammadan States of India. 12 plates.

(92) British Museum Catalogue: Mogul Emperors. 33 plates.

(93) A New Find of Early Muhammadan Coins. Dr. Hoernle. 4 plates

(94) Notes on Copper Buddhist Coins. H. Rivett-Carnac. 2 plates.

(95) Ancient Copper Coins of Kashmir. Dr. Hoernle. 1 plate.

(96) Coins of Modern Native Chiefs of the Punjab. Major Temple. 2 plates.

(97) Notes on the Mint Towns and Coins of the Muhammadans. By Eugene Leggett. 2 maps.

(98) Zoroastrian Deities on Indo-Scythian Coins. Dr. A. Stein. 1 plate.

(99) Symbols on Punch-marked Coins. W. Theobold. 4 plates.

(100) Notes on Gupta Coins. By E. J. Rapson. 1 plate.

(101) The Currencies of Rajputana. Surgeon-Capt. W. W. Webb. 12 plates and map.

Besides these there are many books and papers on Northern India coins in French, German and Russian.

INDEX.